The Art of Freestyle

Eric Brymer, Tom Hughes
and
Loel Collins

Pesda Press – Wales

First published in Great Britain 2000
by Pesda Press
'Elidir'
Ffordd Llanllechid
Rachub
Bangor
Gwynedd
LL57 3EE

ISBN   0 - 9531956 - 3 - 5

Design and layout - Franco Ferrero

Printed by Cambrian Printers - Wales

Foreword

Never before has so much freestyle, rodeo and playboating information from so many great boaters been gathered together in one place.

In a world dominated by the biggest, the fastest, the loudest... the most big headed, this book makes a stand. Whilst of course covering all the latest moves, the authors have not been frightened to start right back at basic concepts. Technical ability is nothing without knowledge, without planning and without stamina. This book tells you the secrets.

Freestyle is a thinking person's sport. The authors, the contributors and the book's publisher have an unrivalled breadth of knowledge in this field, so let this book do some of the thinking for you. The full colour format and the emphasis on personal training and coaching make for a particularly easy read.

When planning my preparation or training before a competition, I always try to evaluate its potential benefits in terms of how many places it will have helped me move up in the final results. As a general rule in life, any time spent off the water should be viewed with suspicion! However, use this time constructively and absorb the information in this book and you will reap your own rewards.

The Art of Freestyle is a book genuinely written by paddlers for paddlers. It is often a hard task to get top athletes to part with their preferred training or competition techniques, but this book is full of such 'Top Tips'. This is not a book written just by its authors, but by a wealth of accomplished paddlers. It is this subtle combination that keeps the reader in the real world... believing in a move, not just imagining it. This is the real world... believe you can do it.

Shaun Baker.

About the Authors

Eric Brymer

Eric's initial involvement in coaching and sport science was as a direct result of developing fitness routines and effective nutrition habits for a variety of athletic disciplines. This interest in fitness led to his involvement in the setting up of facilities in America, Europe and the UK.

As a competitive coach he initially became involved with sports such as gymnastics and swimming. Eventually he discovered kayaking and canoeing in 1990 and has been coaching the sport ever since.

Today his involvement is more specifically with coaching white water freestyle for the Welsh Elite Squad. He has a degree in Sport Science and a postgraduate interest in Sport Psychology. He is also a Master Practitioner in Neuro-Linguistic Programming (NLP) and trained in Hypnosis and Kinesiology. When not coaching freestyle he works as a personal, professional and organisational development coach.

Loel Collins

Loel works as the Director of the National Whitewater Centre in North Wales. He competed in the Freestyle World Championships held on the Ocoee River in the USA and coached members of the UK squad for the following World Championship in Augsburg. He is one of the UK's most qualified coaches and was one of the first to specialise in coaching freestyle, developing many of the strategies in use today.

'Magic' Tom Hughes

Tom just goes boating... A lot!

Contents

Part Three Training for Freestyle

Appendices

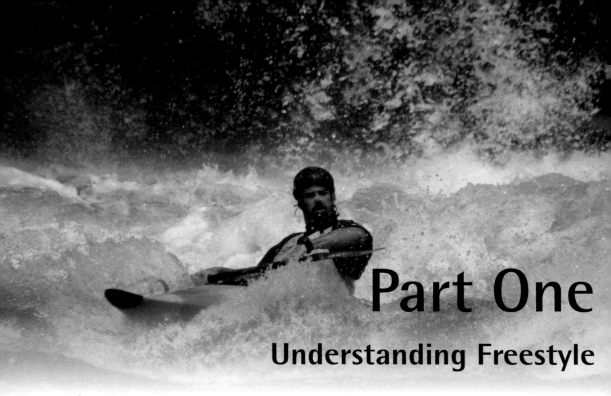

Part One

Understanding Freestyle

The origins of freestyle kayaking lie in obscurity; no one seems to know for sure where and when it started. One rumour has it that freestyle started when a group of Grand Canyon safety kayakers tried to make good on the warranty of their Iliads, another that it came about from watching and imitating particularly impressive trashings on the East Coast of the USA.

Whatever its origins, it is an acknowledged fact that freestyle is one of the most impressive forms of paddlesport. It has breathed new life and individuality into a sport that was suffering from the mundane routines of slalom training or the excessive adrenaline and hairy machismo of river running. Hey... but then everyone thinks their discipline is what God would be doing on his day off!

Perhaps the best way to understand the intricacies of freestyle kayaking is to look at the sport through its more commonly known alias: playboating. Note that the emphasis in all of freestyle kayaking is the word 'play'. Whether you are simply playing on your local river with a few friends or aspire to greatness at the next world championship, this book is designed for you.

The assumption is made that to even begin to playboat, the paddler will already be an intermediate white water paddler who is familiar with the basic strokes and boating skills. For the interested non paddler a glossary is included.

Part One introduces the subject as well as exploring safety issues and key concepts. Part Two describes the moves in detail. Part Three shows us how to train in order to hone our physical and mental skills and be 'the best we can be'.

But remember, it should always be play. As soon as you start to forget this you are forgetting the very reason why you surely took up kayaking in the first place.

"Go play the river."

1 Equipment

Before you even start to think of progressing in freestyle, it is a good idea to take a long, analytical look at your equipment. If you have gear that you are comfortable using, your progression in the sport will be quicker and less strenuous. This is *not* to say that aspiring freestylers should go out and spend hard earned cash on all the latest equipment, but that when purchasing a new piece of kit, bear in mind the purpose for which you intend to use it.

One of the most important purchases you will make, and without doubt the most expensive, is your boat. Let's dwell for a while on the features of freestyle kayaks.

Boats

Boat design is being pushed to the limit by freestyle kayaking. Hardly a month goes by without a boat designer introducing a new and often confusing innovation into the market place. Freestyle boats are probably best divided into generations which have broadly similar design features:

First Generation

When freestyle first took off it was known as 'Hot Dogging', and competitions were known as 'Rodeos' (this latter term is still commonly used). Boats were broadly speaking river running designs which either allowed 'Big Air Time' during pop outs, or manoeuvrability while in a hole. High volume kayaks such as the Corsica or the Aeroquatic were very popular for air time, while shorter boats (most notably the 'Spud' or Topolino) were fun in shallower holes. During this era, judging was informal and moves done during competition were reasonably simple, so Rodeo was as much a competition involving personality and finesse as it was about boat control.

Second Generation

Germany's Prijon company broke the mould when it introduced a radical boat designed primarily for the growing freestyle market. They were soon followed by other boat manufacturers, and boats such as the Hurricane (Avenger), Dagger Transition and Pyranha Acrobat

Pyranha Acrobat 300, second generation

300 (the latter two in very early prototype form), swept the board at the Ocoee World Championships. Since these new boats were radical they allowed a new breed of freestyle move to be developed, and boat control advanced to the realms of the vertical plane. For the first time cartwheels were commonly seen at British Rodeos.

Third Generation

The two years following the Ocoee Worlds saw a period of great development in both boat design and the moves done in those boats. They generally became shorter, and had flat backs and sharper rails to allow slicing during repeated cartwheels. The Eskimo Kendo, Acrobat 270, Dagger RPM and Perception Whippit are all typical designs from this era.

Fourth Generation

Again boats became shorter, enabling holes to be retained more easily. Volume was once again reduced, with very sharp rails allowing vertical moves even away from white water features. As a general rule hulls became flatter, 'wave moves' more popular and verticality on waves more feasible. Typical examples of these boats are the Wavesport Stubby, Pyranha Storm, Dagger Vertigo and Riot 007.

Fifth Generation

As we enter the new millennium change is happening at a frenetic pace. This is due to the increasing popularity of 'wave moves', and the fact that manufacturers respond to each new vogue with increasing rapidity. The Riot Glide, Wavesport X and Dagger Mediaeval are all typical of fifth generation boats. They have sharp edges, reasonably long length compared to the previous generation and, most importantly, specially designed hulls that surpass earlier ones since they comprise a number of features designed to make them 'looser' on a wave.

Wavesport Forplay, sixth generation

'Loose' is an expression that comes from surfing, and refers to the ease with which the stern of the kayak slips from under you whilst surfing across a wave. In this context it indicates the ease with which a boat can be spun in the flat plane whilst on a wave.

Sixth Generation

During the writing of this book fifth generation kayaks have been surpassed by their smaller cousins, the sixth generation boats. Boats such as the Wavesport XXX, Dagger Vengeance and Perception Mr. Clean, show design features of extreme low volume combined with wave surfing features that may herald the beginning of a new playboating age. Broadly speaking they share similar features such as very low volume ends, extremely sharp rails and a considerable amount of volume toward the cockpit. This makes the cockpit area of such boats look very much like, as a friend of mine put it, "a tank turret".

Choosing a Boat

Choosing the boat for you is a difficult and frequently expensive exercise. If you are a novice to freestyle then an earlier generation boat may suffice for now. However, there is

Photos
Top Left - Pyranha acrobat 270, third generation
Middle Left - Wavesport Stubby, fourth generation
Bottom Left - Riot Glide, fifth generation

little point spending good money on a second hand boat, only to find that you rapidly outperform your boat, and are frustrated by the limitations of the older generation kayaks.

More advanced paddlers will probably want a more recent design, but be warned... It is better to practice in a boat in which you are completely happy than to go out and buy the latest model in the mistaken belief that the design of the boat will compensate for flaws in your technique. However, if you are aspiring to the latest moves then it is really the latest playboat that you want; green spins on a wave are much easier when your boat is designed for that purpose.

What to Look for When Buying a Freestyle Boat

What with the bewildering variety of boats on the market, it is useful to think about a number of factors before parting with your cash:

1. Are you comfortable? Many modern freestyle boats lack in foot room what they make up for in performance. After all, Ferraris aren't really the most comfortable cars are they? Despite the fact that your possible purchase is excellent for all the latest moves, you may not be able to stay in it for long. If this is the case then it is probably better to go for a slightly larger option. Freestyle kayaking requires considerable amounts of practice time, and if you cannot practice comfortably then your performance will be inhibited. Another important consideration is whether there is sufficient volume behind the seat to ensure that, when working on tail moves, you are not lying with your back deep in the water.

Performer's Top Tip

I was paddling a mother ship called the Hurricane back in 1996 on the Rabioux Wave, and I was playing hard, but the boats we had were too big for us. The designs were really old, so we didn't progress so quickly and it took me two years to learn to cartwheel. A year later I went to Canada, and Chan from Wavesport gave me a Stubby to bring back to the UK; from this time on I had a boat that was smaller and fitted me better, and I started to improve. In one season I went from flat spins on one side to eight point cartwheels on my left and for ever on my right! The boats got smaller and smaller, so smaller people could throw them around... Choose the right boat, don't go for a boat which is just too big.

Deb Pinniger is the current (1999) Ladies Freestyle Kayak World Champion, full time paddler and member of Team Wavesport.

2. Can your purchase do the moves that you want to do? Although many manufacturers claim that their boats can do all the latest moves, the reality is that some of them cannot. Watch other boaters. What boats are they using? How are they performing? Can they achieve the moves that they are going for?

   This point is particularly true since the dawn of newer wave moves and the advent of flat hulls. Some hulls are 'looser' on the wave than others and can consequently spin and blunt with greater ease. If you want to do these moves then the 'looser' your hull the greater your chance of success.

3. Can you perform to the capabilities of the kayak? This does *not* mean can you jump in the boat and immediately start to shred waves in it, but rather, can you do basic river skills in your chosen boat. Can you roll it easily one hundred per cent of the time (or near enough)? Can you ferryglide in it without catching the edge and flipping? Does the boat feel unstable?... If you feel that the boat may be too radical for you then it's definitely best to get another boat; you don't want any embarrassing wet exits.

4. Can you hold the boat on edge comfortably? A large percentage of freestyle moves (a year or so ago I would have written 'majority', but that goes to show how fast the sport is progressing), involve holding the kayak on its edge. If you find it hard to tilt the boat onto its side or feel really unstable when doing so, it's a fair bet that your prospective purchase is not the boat for you. Go back to the shop and ask to try another one.

Buy the boat that suits *you* best, not the one your friends think is the coolest or has the nicest colour scheme. After all, it's you who is going to be paddling it.

Paddles

Probably the most personal piece of kit a kayaker purchases is a set of blades. You will frequently find kayakers willing to let you try their boats, but rarely will a paddler allow you to sample his or her paddles. For freestyle paddling it is a good idea to use paddles that are light and responsive. Metal edged clubs are well and truly out since they are too rigid, heavy and slow for most freestyle paddlers.

Describing Paddles

For the purposes of this book I have used the following terms to describe particular parts of paddles:

The *drive face* is the concave side of the blade. The side of the blade which engages the water when you are paddling forwards. (Sometimes known as the power face).

The *reverse face* is the convex side of the blade. This is usually the side of the blade which you will place on the water for support when side surfing on a *low brace*.

The *shaft* is the long, oval tube that joins the two blades together.

Shaft

Many freestyle kayakers prefer paddles on a carbon, composite or glass shaft. These allow greater responsiveness and contact with the water, as well as being lighter and strong enough to be relied upon in heavy water conditions. You can almost *feel* the water better when using these.

Overgripping the paddles blocks feedback and encourages injury. The correct equipment is essential and this should include some surfers' wax for the shaft. This is rubbed onto the shaft and makes it 'tacky', increasing the apparent grip and reducing the paddler's psychological need to grip the shaft so tightly.

Blade Shape

Blades can be referred to as either symmetric or asymmetric. Asymmetric blades are better suited for freestyle paddling for two reasons:

1. They behave well in the water, i.e. they don't 'wobble' when you pull them through the water. Symmetric blades do wobble, and to compensate for this the paddler will grip the shaft tightly. This increases the possibility of wrist injury, and prevents the paddler from getting true feedback from the paddles as they slice and manoeuvre through the water.

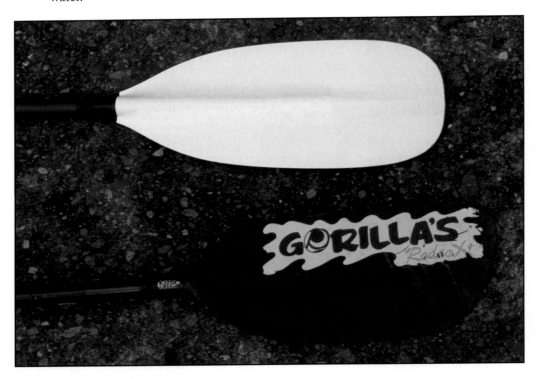

Symmetric (top) and asymmetric (bottom) blades

2. Asymmetric blades enter and exit the water cleanly, i.e. with less turbulence. This speeds up the paddle rate and the ease with which strokes can be linked together.

Feather

Blade feather (the degree to which blades are offset from one another), is largely a matter of personal choice. I personally use blades set at 45° and know few boaters who use a feather exceeding 60°. Not only does this reduced feather allow faster stroke repetition, but reduces the danger of a paddler developing inflammation of the wrist known as tendinitis. Another handy side effect of using paddles with very little feather is that you can use both blades to push down on the water when doing some vertical moves, providing a limited degree of stability on both sides of the kayak at the same time.

Some element of feather is needed because, when you pull and push the paddle about, a feathered paddle allows the wrists to maintain an (anatomically speaking), stronger position.

Clothing

There is a plethora of clothing available designed with the freestyle market in mind, and kayaking has for the first time become almost as fashion orientated as it has practical. The main consideration is the practicality of your clothing. Freestyle requires complex strokes and radical body twists, so it is a good idea to buy paddle wear that allows considerable freedom of movement, but provides enough support to avoid injury. Even expert freestylers spend considerable amounts of time immersed in cold water, so warmth is a priority (especially in Britain). Since success requires a great deal of practice, and freestyle paddling is dangerously addictive, you should take a careful look at the build quality of your kit. Nothing is more annoying than a cold day spent performing below par due to failures in equipment.

Different priorities! - Danny Noblett (left) and Nick Targett

Spraydecks

This is without doubt the most important purchase you will make when buying a piece of gear. It is possible (just about) to spend a day playboating in inferior clothing, but an inferior spraydeck will eventually lead to an embarrassing and unnecessary wet exit. Make sure that your spraydeck fits your boat correctly and is not so tight around your waist as to restrict breathing. After all, cardiovascular sports are much harder to do when you are suffocating! Recommended spraydecks are usually neoprene and almost completely exclude water seepage. Make sure that you can get the spraydeck off in an emergency, and that your grab loop (if you have had your present deck for a long time), has not frayed or looks worn. I've seen some very old grab loops snap just when the boater really wanted out.

Cags

For cold water kayaking or freestyle which requires constant immersion, it is a good idea to buy a 'dry' cag from a well known manufacturer. Your neck seal should be as comfortable as possible and arms should allow plenty of movement without being inconveniently baggy.

Buoyancy Aids

Freedom of movement is a priority here. Your old river running buoyancy aid, complete with throw bag pockets and chest harness is probably too cumbersome for the radical paddle strokes needed in freestyle. Check that there is no restriction to arm movement and that the buoyancy does not ride up while sitting in a boat, or even worse, swimming down the river.

Remember that too much buoyancy in your jacket may become as much an inconvenience as too little. I have seen many kayakers for whom capsizing is almost an impossibility due to excessive flotation in their jackets.

Under/Layered Wear

I am reluctant to comment on the various merits offered by clothes worn under conventional paddle wear. Whilst wetsuits are warm, they are often constrictive and dry suits often have harsh zip systems which restrict movement further. Warm and comfortable is a convenient guideline.

Helmets

Fashion has lately led to many kayakers wearing carbon brain buckets. They are light, cool looking and easy to get hold of *but* offer little protection on impact with nasty rocks. Another matter of personal choice, but remember: it is a good idea to be able to see where you are going, prevention of impact being better than cure!

Recent rumour has it that competitive paddlers must soon only wear helmets that are C.E.N. approved; no point spending money on a helmet that you'll have to get rid of if you start to compete seriously.

Health Check

Playboating is a wet sport and we all spend a lot of time upside down! Repeated immersion forces cold water in and out of the ear canal; ultimately this can lead to the development of a bony growth across the ear canal... Not good! To reduce the risk of this, all paddlers should wear a skull cap that covers the ears, or good silicone ear plugs. You should also get your ears checked by a doctor regularly. It's either that or only paddle when the water is warm!

2 Hydrology

Warning! Reading this chapter may increase your life expectancy considerably.

Before you begin to learn anything about freestyle kayaking it is wise to have a think about some of the forces you will be playing with. You will never understand the principles behind the moves described further on in this book without a brief overview of the playing ground... you wouldn't play golf without understanding about greens, holes and bunkers now, would you?

Green Water

Green water is any water that is flowing downstream under the actual surface of the river. Examples of green water include water that flows *underneath* holes and pushes you out of them when you are upside down. Another example is all the water that combines to make up that lovely glassy surf wave, except the very surface of the wave. If you allow your boat's edge to plunge beneath the surface of the wave during a flat spin, this edge will catch the green water and will be carried downstream; you will follow, upright or otherwise.

Eddies

As the river rushes downhill it will occasionally come up against a solid object such as a rock or part of the river bank. Since this object is solid and water is liquid (bit of a no-brainer eh!), the river will flow around the rock. Most of the water that flows around a rock continues downstream, but some turns back upstream and fills in the void left behind the rock. The water behind rocks, therefore, is flowing upstream (another no-brainer), and these upstream flowing areas are called eddies!

Eddy Fences

Eddy lines or fences are the areas where the upstream flowing water of the eddy is next to the downstream flowing water of the rest of the river. They often have areas of 'funny water', and small whirlpools may often travel along them. Don't worry though, they are excellent places for playboating!

On very high volume rivers there is extreme turbulence on eddy lines and they tend to become vicious, nasty places with large whirlpools and strange hydraulics that can sometimes suck boats down! These are not excellent places for playboating!

Cushions

Remember the solid object that created the eddy? Well, because water piles up on the upstream side of this object, a thing called a cushion is created. This is just what it sounds like, a large cushion of water (usually, but not always broken) on the upstream side of a rock. A cushion really acts as a natural deflector for the solid object but is often used by playboaters for fun. Remember though, the existence of a cushion does not guarantee a safe splat rock.

Waves

Waves on a river are very similar to waves you would find in the ocean, the only difference being that on an ocean wave the water stays still and the wave moves, whereas on a river the wave stays in the same place and the water moves.

There are various features of a river wave; the terminology of these should be understood before you read the wave move chapters of this book.

Ramp

This is the ramp of water that falls from upstream into the wave; ideally the ramp will be very smooth and unbroken, to form that perfect smooth wave.

Features of a wave - Pete Astles, Skookumchuck, Canada - Photo: Matt Stephens, Peak UK

Face
The upstream part of the wave which faces the ramp forming it.

Trough
This is the lowest (and fastest) part of the wave, right at the bottom of the face.

Peak
The top of the face, actually the slowest part of the wave but the place from which you will ideally initiate most surfing moves.

Back
This is the part of the wave that faces downstream, usually seen from downstream as a hump, as you fall off the back of that perfect wave you just missed!

Broken Waves
Broken waves are waves where underwater turbulence or a confused ramp lead to a broken rather than glassy face. Quite often the break can be found right on the peak of the wave and can be used almost like a stopper to initiate flat spins or to prevent you from falling off the back.

Breaking Waves
On high volume rivers some waves tend to surge, just like they do in the surf. While riding one of these waves you can perform most of the usual freestyle tricks but it is a good idea to be quite low down the face, or even out-running the wave by riding up the ramp, when the wave eventually surges so that it breaks.

Holes and Stoppers
Holes can either be your best friend or your worst enemy; recognition of each type is one of the keys to freestyle success. Before we start to look at what to avoid let's look at what we need to play with.

Again, there are certain features of a hole which should be recognised before we go into the detail of freestyle moves:

Ramp
Just like surf waves, holes have their own ramps. It is the ramp of water falling down from upstream that creates the hole. Holes with extremely steep ramps are known as 'pourovers' and tend to be either good fun or truly nasty.

Pile
This is the confused mass of white water which constitutes the hole's face. Pile, however, does not simply refer to the side of the hole facing upstream, (as face does with a wave), but the whole of the broken section of water. This is because all the water upstream of the boil line is flowing back into the hole, even where its surface is angled downstream. It is therefore possible to retain (not get swept out of) the hole from that part of the pile which is angled downstream but which is still sucking you upstream and further into the hole.

Boil Line
The boil line is an area of confused water downstream of the pile, where the green water that has charged under the pile resurfaces, creating something similar to an eddy fence. By

learning to look at boil lines it becomes possible for you to tell whether the hole is friendly (a 'playhole') or liable to trap and work you. If the boil line is more than a boat length away from the trough (see below), then it's probably best to leave the hole alone for a while, or at least to persuade the blind probe in your group to check it out first.

Trough

This is the place where the green water rushing down the ramp collides with the pile pushing back upstream. Usually there is a clearly defined area here known as the 'maw', 'squeeze', 'slot' or 'trough' where the two contradictory river forces actually meet.

Green Water (see earlier notes)

The solid mass of water rushing under the hole. You want to catch a small bit of green water with the edge of your boat during a cartwheel, or stick a hell of a lot of any surface area into the green water to escape the clutches of that surprisingly powerful hole you didn't want to be in.

Kick

Every hole has a certain direction in which it is 'kicking'. This means that if the kick of the hole is to the left then boaters playing in the hole will be pushed to the left hand side of

Features of a hole   -   'Fast' Eddy Cleaton, River Lothar, Austria

the hole and will usually exit on this side. Usually the direction of kick is towards the side of the hole which has the most green water pushing past it.

The Difference Between a 'Good' and a 'Bad' Hole

There is no foolproof formula for deciding whether a hole is playful or horrible. Indeed I have often heard it said that one man's playhole is another's washing machine from hell. There are however a number of pointers that may help you steer clear of the nasties:

1. *Ramp angle* - If the angle of the hole's ramp is steep then the hole becomes known as a pourover. Because you want to keep your upstream edges clear of the green water when side surfing, you have to edge your boat excessively when in a pourover. This can lead to difficult braces and potential workings. Avoid pourovers which have a very steep angle or a high volume of water piling over them.

2. *Boil line* - If the boil line of the hole is more than a boat length from the trough itself, it is likely that the hole will recirculate (keep in and wash around) a swimmer, and may be difficult to exit while in your boat. Treat this type of hole with respect.

3. *Angle of the ends* - If the ends of the hole point upstream then the direction of 'kick' is likely to be back upstream as well; this will give the hole a horseshoe type appearance with the base of the 'U' pointing downstream. This will make it difficult to either punch through the hole or to exit the hole at its sides.

4. *Depth* - It is probably best to avoid a hole if it is particularly shallow, or even worse has an inconveniently placed rock. Power flipping in shallow holes increases the chances of injury.

Things to Look for in a Good Hole:

1. *Other boaters* - Let's face it, in most places where there is a good playhole there will already be other kayakers. Watch them, how do they enter the hole? What moves are they going for? How do they get out of it?

2. *Angle of ramp* - Really good playholes tend to have a very gently angled ramp; sometimes these ramps are so nicely angled that you hardly need to support on your blades at all to remain upright in the hole. This forgiving angle allows you to concentrate more on your position in the hole than on staying upright, allowing you to work harder to get the moves instead of struggling with the lack of stability.

3. *An attainable exit* - If the ends of the hole are angled downstream from the trough, you can probably work your way toward them with assertive forward or backward strokes, and punch your way out of the sides. You may also find that you are carried along to one of these ends during the process of side surfing by the hole's kick. If the sides of your hole are closed off, as in a low head dam or a weir, don't even think about playing there. There is a fine line between playing and getting played with.

4. *Depth* - An ideal hole will be deep and retentive enough to allow cartwheels, but forgiving enough that you wash out of the hole when you are upside down for an extended time. Check out the distance from the trough to the boil line for an indication of whether this is likely to happen.

5. *Run out* - Does the hole have a deep calm pool running out of it in which to roll up? If not, are you sure you can roll in time?

3 Hole Escape Strategies

"How to get out of holes? Don't go in them, very simple." Dave
Manby, Coruh River Trips.

We all make mistakes and there will undoubtedly come a time when you drop into a hole
that is a little too powerful for you, so it's a good idea to think about some of the emergency
procedures that *may* help you get out of that non comedy moment.

Dropping In

The first few milliseconds when you drop into a nasty hole can make the difference
between a skin of the teeth incident and a complete trashing. If you drop in sideways you are
most likely to stay in the hole in a side surf position. *Lean forward* and keep your paddles in
a *low brace position* (see title photo). Then, if the unthinkable happens and you power flip on
entry, your shoulders are protected and your body is loose enough to respond.

Punching Holes

As soon as you realise that the hole is nastier than you first expected (hopefully before you
are actually side surfing), turn your boat to face downstream and get in a few good solid
paddle strokes toward the area of the hole which looks most as though it is flushing through
(with any luck it'll be a tongue of green water). As soon as you hit the hole keep your weight
forward and *keep paddling*; by tucking forward you will present less surface area to the hole
and may be able to squeeze underneath the pile.

If you have a tendency to back loop when punching holes, think about lifting one of your
knees slightly as you hit the pile. By doing this you will reduce the surface area of your stern
so that it is less likely to be caught by the green water of the ramp, and also aid the stern in
shedding water. Another advantage of this slight tilt is that it sets up pre-rotation so that you
can screw up out of the back loop really fast if it still happens!

Catching some of the green water on the hole's ramp before you actually hit the hole may
be worth a try if you are confident you can roll once in the hole. I have seen people tail squirt

before hitting the pile using the stern to catch green water and pull them through. Even more radically, it may be possible to roll under the hole by capsizing deliberately on the ramp, surely only a strategy for true emergencies?

Coach's Top Tip

When you are thinking about getting into that hole... take the time to have a good look at it. The features you need to check out from a 'How do I get out of that' point of view, are the same ones you need to understand in order to make the most of the hole's freestyle potential. To quote a jet fighter test pilot: "Never put your body where your mind hasn't been first".

Franco Ferrero is a BCU Level 5 Coach, the author of 'White Water Safety and Rescue' and the owner of Pesda Press.

Getting Stuck

Eventually you will wind up side surfing and getting a good 'trashing'. This is the River God's way of reminding you who is in charge; just accept it but remember the River God will only help those that help themselves. There are two general rules to making a trashing less severe and 'getting away with it'.

Rule One – Keep Moving

In nearly every kayak video there is an out-takes section. Watch it carefully and try and work out what most people do to extricate themselves from a 'trashing'... in most cases it isn't much! Many unenlightened people still seem to work on the theory that if you just hang in there long enough you will eventually get out.

Keep moving doesn't just mean keep moving so that you are upright. Keep the bow of the boat moving, try one end of the hole and, if that doesn't work, back paddle to the other end. Failing to get out of the hole at either end usually means that you will have to bring Rule Two into play.

Rule Two – Green Water

In most cases where you are trying to get out of the hole the green water is your friend. Try and present as much surface area to the green water as possible; usually the green water will grab this surface area and sweep it out of the hole. There are numerous ways of doing this:

Hanging In

If you find yourself upside down in the hole, don't roll too quickly. With a bit of luck your body or paddles will act as a water anchor, get hooked by the green water flowing under the hole, and be pulled downstream.

Endos

If you find yourself horizontal to the hole, try dropping either end of the boat into the green water as you would for a front or back loop. The surface area of the ends of your boat may be enough to snag that precious green, and you're out of there!

Ends

If you can't quite work the boat to the ends of the hole and get released, you'll often find that the boat turns as it would during a 360° spin in a hole. As soon as you are facing downstream at the side of the hole (but not quite out of it), try capsizing into the green water rushing past the side. Luck may cause your body or paddles to land in this rushing water and you'll be pulled out of the hole. Hurrah!

Blasting

In holes with a gentle ramp, but where the sides of the hole are further upstream than the trough, it may be possible to ride up the ramp as you would in a blast and punch your way out of the side. By dropping down the pile as you build up to this, you may develop enough momentum to get out of the hole.

There is no unworthy hole escape strategy except ones that do not work. If you insist on getting out of the hole using some of your freestyle repertoire then try to build up speed while doing so. There is one almost infallible rule... the harder you try to get out of the hole, the harder it is to get out; the harder you try to stay in the hole and play, the easier it is to blow out!

Swimming Out

If you do make the decision to swim out of a hole it is probably better to do it sooner rather than later. There is no point fighting a blood and guts battle to avoid swimming, only to find that when you do eventually swim you have no energy left for the rather more damp battle to follow.

4 Understanding Freestyle

There are four essential prerequisites to speedy advance in freestyle kayaking. When analysing your own performance or asking yourself, "How do they do it?", it is handy and quite simple to think in terms of *Body, Boat, Blade* and *Brain*. This means that when training you should ask yourself, "What am I doing with my body?", "What is my boat *actually* doing?" (as opposed to how I perceive what it is doing), "What am I doing with my blades?".

A good illustration is of a triangle in which the base is the body. The boat and blade support each other, and in turn are both supported by the body. A triangle is fundamentally a strong shape and illustrates the strength in a combination rather than isolation. The brain is the core of the structure; without it the triangle has no substance.(See page 26).

Brain

Possibly the most neglected of these prerequisites is the brain. When you analyse the elements of your performance that come under this heading, brain can refer to mental preparation or tactics.

Mental Preparation

In freestyle kayaking there are a number of psychological approaches which can enhance performance which are covered in detail in Part Three. However, the one approach that you will need to engage right from the start is Positive Mental Attitude, as well as a willingness to learn.

Tactics

This is your understanding of how the move is performed, what is actually possible on a given river feature, how to set up for a sequence, or where the 'sweet spot' is that will allow you to pull off a given move.

Coaching Matrices

A freestyle run contains three elements: Start - Content - Finish.

The start and finish of any run can be pro-active whilst the content of a run needs to be both pro and re-active. This exercise can be completed at two levels:

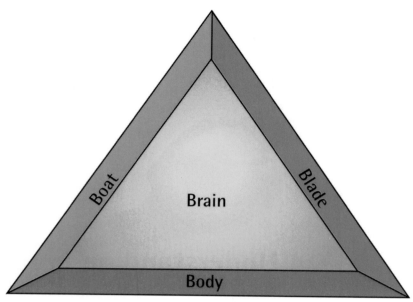

The Four 'B's

1. Initially at a generic level where you as a paddler work out everything you can possibly do.
2. At a level specific to the site you are 'working on'.

Simply split a sheet into three columns:

Column One contains every possible way to get onto the wave.

Column Two contains everything that can go into a run, and can be divided into everything you initiate (pro-active), and everything the water might initiate (partially re-active).

Column Three has everything you could do to end the run.

Once the sheets have been prepared, runs can be choreographed both practically as part of a goal setting process and as part of a mental rehearsal tool. (See Chapter 10.2).

Start	Content	Finish
Paddle on L/R	Surf upstream	Wash off
Tail squirt on L	Reverse surf	Loop off
Cartwheel on L	Cartwheel L/R	360 off
Reverse on L/R	Reverse surf	720 off
Drop in L/R	Flat 360	Cartwheel off
Blast on L	Flat 180	Tail squirt off
	Power flip	Roll off

Example of a coaching matrix put together for a specific paddler on a specific site.

Choreography

Another consideration when choreographing runs is to consider the content of the run in broader terms. Choreograph your runs to fulfil as many of the criteria listed below as you can. Judges will mark the choreographed moves subconsciously; and the crowd will be far more impressed than they would be by a series of unconnected but technically high scoring moves. A good run must contain:

- Changes in direction
- Changes in speed
- Changes in height

It should also:

- Be fluent
- Use the entire rapid
- Have a variety of manoeuvres both left and right

Body

During the course of Part Two we will be breaking down many of the freestyle moves into component parts. There are however general concepts that may help your progression in freestyle. In terms of the body, some of these are:

Posture

The sitting position in a kayak is not good for your posture. The position of the back whilst sitting down creates stresses along the back that are potentially dangerous for the paddler. The twists and turns of paddling only serve to compound any problem, so it is important to identify a suitable posture that the paddler can assume and the actions that are least likely to risk injury.

Whilst standing, the back has four curves in it. These form an inward curve at the neck, an outward curve at the top of the back, an inward curve in the small of the back, and a final outward curve at its base.

Whilst in this position the back could be described as being 'in balance'; i.e. the components of vertebrae and cartilage all sit in position as they were designed to do. However, whilst sitting the curves in the back are lost and the spine is straightened. The vertebrae, being bone, do not bend to accommodate this. The flex is accommodated in the cartilage. The effect is to squeeze the cartilage into a wedge between the vertebrae. Over time, the firmer 'core' of the cartilage can be displaced and can apply pressure to the nerves that leave the vertebrae and create problems. If 'shocked' this can result in a slipped or 'prolapsed disc'.

The sitting position is difficult to alter, but certain basic posture considerations can help:

1. Keep your head up. Many people will lower their head when they want to paddle more powerfully; this accentuates the loss of the curve in the neck.
   "Head up, you're proud to be a paddler."
2. The hunched white water tyro stance, likewise, accentuates the loss of the small of the back, (it also restricts breathing). So sit upright.
   "Paddle like a giraffe."

A series of exercises as part of the warm down can also be used to redress the imbalance created by the sitting position. These stretch the back in the opposite direction. (See Chapter 8.3 and 9.3)

Posture and Technique

Whilst sitting in the kayak, the hips can be flexed from side to side. If the paddler leans backwards, the back is placed in such a position that the hips cannot be moved, and shifting the upper body from side to side becomes the only way to control boat balance. For this reason an upright posture is encouraged; the successful control being created by the flex of the hips rather than weight shift. This involves far less effort.

Centre of Gravity (Static Balance)

Try and keep you body weight over the kayak as much as possible. One useful example of this is when you are holding the boat on edge; edging the boat is *not* the same as when you practise support strokes in a swimming pool. In such exercises (especially when you are first learning to kayak) the body will often be out to the side of the kayak with most, or all, of the body weight loaded onto the paddle which you are using to push you back upright.

When *edging* however, your hips tilt toward the higher edge of the kayak and keep your centre of gravity over the kayak as much as possible. By keeping your centre of gravity over the kayak, you increase your stability (even while on edge), and consequently maintain control of the boat throughout the whole sequence.

Static balance, edging - Bleddyn Lloyd, Chapel Falls, Canolfan Tryweryn.

Centre of Gravity (Dynamic Balance)

When the boat is stationary, or slow moving, balance can only be achieved by using knees, hips and buttocks and keeping the centre of gravity inside the boat. As the boat moves progressively faster into turns, the centre of gravity can be shifted outside the boat, allowing you to lean, like a motor biker taking a bend at speed. The faster the boat is moving relative to the water, the more weight can be moved outside the boat.

Dynamic balance - Paul 'Cheesy' Robertson, Full James NZ - Photo: Jason Smith / Pyranha

Direction of Head Turn

Look where you want to be as *long as possible*. For example when cartwheeling, don't look over the downstream shoulder early, because that is precisely where you will go. Keep your gaze focused where you want to land the end of your kayak next, and you will (usually) land it there. In a cartwheel this will mean looking over your upstream shoulder as long as you can, even when the bow of your boat is rotating underwater to point downstream.

That said, looking to a point won't, of itself, drag the boat to that point. The start of the sequence has to be correct and you have to know what you are trying to achieve. This 'looking to future water', as the squirt boys say, works best with some degree of visualisation skill, (see Chapter 10.2).

Looking for the next move - Simon Westgarth, Hurley Weir

Boat

When competing in freestyle competition, it is the cavorting of the boat on the wave or hole that scores nearly all your points. Think about how to get the best out of your boat and how you can improve its performance.

Padding

It may sound obvious but it still amazes me how many people paddle kayaks that are little more than factory produced shells. Manufacturers try their best to make their kayaks as user

Performer's Top Tip

You've gotta have dreadlocks and throw them around! Use your head and your shoulders, throw them around and your boat will follow.

Allan Ellard was a member of the British Rodeo Squad at the 1997 Ottawa World Championships. He is sponsored by Pyranha, Robson and Canyon Gear.

friendly as possible but, no matter what shape you are, your boat will need some form of additional padding to customise it for you.

Ideally you should have six areas of contact between your body and your kayak:

1. The first of these is obviously your buttocks; you do sit in the kayak after all! Make sure your seat is padded comfortably.
2. Take a good look at your backrest; if it doesn't provide enough support then go at it with some close celled foam from a camper mat.
3. Thigh / knee braces should be tailored to your leg length by adjusting them if they are adjustable, and padding out with closed cell foam if they are not.
4. Your footrest should be the next port of call; if it's too loose you'll get no feel from it, too tight and the boat will be uncomfortable.
5. Now think about your ankles (especially in modern playboats). Do they rub against the kayak? Is there a case for padding out some ankle support?
6. Finally think about your hip pads. Many boaters simply use these to cushion river running bumps, but since freestyle moves rely on considerable hip control you should really pad them out to get maximum performance. Ideally they should lock you into your kayak without preventing an emergency exit or becoming uncomfortable.

"A kayak is not something you sit in to travel down rivers, it's something you wear while you dance among the rapids"- Ultimate Descents International - Nepal.

Blades

The complex contortions of blades, so common in freestyle, are often the first stumbling block a newcomer has to overcome. During all kayaking the blades have two purposes: power and support. By keeping the body's centre of gravity over the boat as far as possible,

Or alternatively...

It is not built into my body returning back into holes. There is no reason to look back into a hole other than to go "phew, I just missed it!"

Paul Cripps is co-owner and operator of Amazonas Explorer Rafting based in Cuzco, Peru; he is a well known expedition kayaker with an aversion to playing in holes.

the amount of support you actually need from the blades is kept to a minimum, rather use them to force the ends of the boat down or to initiate the move.

In most instances it is a good idea to keep your blades as close to the surface of the water as possible. For example, when cartwheeling the blade should brace on the surface of the hole's pile. Even when cartwheeling on an eddy line, there is very rarely a need to push the blade very far under the water. You can use the surface tension of the water and the large surface area of the blade to work in your favour without plunging the blade itself very deep at all.

Coaching Point

Complex paddle movements do not, contrary to popular belief, achieve control of the boat by pulling the blade in the water. The blade in the water simply provides a fixed point that the paddler can push against, with his/her feet and knees. For this reason the position of the footrest is important. The paddler should be able to actively push against the footrest.

Observation Skills

Shapes and patterns made by a boat as it travels through the water can provide important clues to the careful observer.

The path of the boat through the water, the way it slides over or cuts through it are all-important. However it's arguably not the boat we watch, but its effect on the water surface.

Wakes at the stern.

1. Alternate sliding from side to side could illustrate the amount of turning effect created in a stroke.

2. 'Skidding' at the stern illustrates the amount of edge being applied.

3. Stern lower than wake could indicate the paddler sits back or the boat is too small.

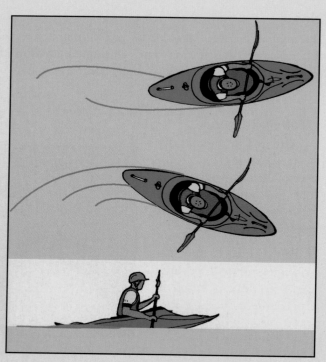

Waves at the bow

1. A large wave right at the bow may suggest the boat is too small, or the paddler is leaning forwards.

2. A wave a long way back could indicate that the seat is too far back or the paddler sits back. The boat could be at maximum speed- no need to paddle any harder.

3. An even wave on the waterline indicates the boat is moving forwards at a constant speed.

4. Waves on alternate sides indicate a turning effect of a stroke.

5. A pulsating wave indicates that the paddler is leaning forwards with each stroke.

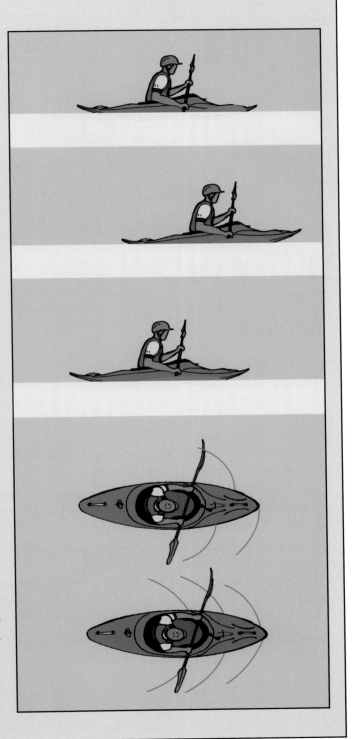

Part Two

The Moves

This part of the book is designed to break down many of the current freestyle moves in an easily understood and uncluttered way. It is divided into moves suitable for intermediate kayakers and moves for 'expert' freestylers who may be progressing onto more technical moves. I have left the 'beginner' well out of this lunacy since by definition the 'beginner' will be busy concentrating on support strokes and swimming down Serpent's Tail, rather than entering the eerie world of the vertical plane.

Each freestyle move is explained in numerous ways: a brief description of the move, a series of photos showing how the move looks, a description of how to do the move and a break down of what the boater is doing in terms of *Body, Boat, Blade and Brain*.

It is sometimes a good idea to 'go back to basics' when attempting a new rodeo trick, so each section will be highlighted with a set of other moves which may have to be 're-learnt' or perfected before progress is made. Don't ever be embarrassed by going back to 'popouts', just because you consider yourself to be a cartwheel kind of boater. The mild 'humiliation' will pay dividends in the end, and besides, it's great fun to go 'old school' for an afternoon.

Firstly however it is a good idea to look at some exercises and drills that can help you on your way...

5 Training Drills

Bench Spinning

Put your boat on a garden table or bench and get in it. You will now start to get curious looks from passers by.

Start the boat spinning by prying with either a forward or reverse stroke on one edge of the bench, and use other forward and reverse sweeps to build up speed. Soon it is possible to spin at a rate of knots and to put the fear of an out of control spinning kayak into your (now plentiful) group of passing critics.

Not only is this a fun warm up but it helps the body get used to the extended sweep strokes needed for moves such as rock spins, green spins and tail squirts. Most people who find it hard to tail squirt are being lazy with their strokes and not reaching far back enough to sweep the boat into a tail squirt.

The Trampoline

Get hold of a trampoline or trampette, your local sports centre usually has a club. Start by just jumping up and down on the tramp looking forward.

Once you get a good bounce and are in the air, look quickly over your shoulder, allow your shoulders to turn also in the direction in which you are looking. Your body will then turn in the direction in which you are looking.

If you don't become addicted to the trampoline and give up kayaking for good, you will soon realise that this is a good exercise for developing your 'pre-rotation'. This simple exercise on the tramp should show why most boaters look over the shoulder in the direction of travel while pirouetting.

That said, research into how we create spinning during moves clearly illustrated that, although the rotation from the head was important, it did not in itself create the rotation. The rotation has to be initiated from a purchase point, in our case, blade against water or boat against water. So don't forget the importance of setting up your move.

See how fast you can spin before falling off the bench! - Greer Mackenzie

The possibilities for 'cross training' using trampolines are almost limitless. Snow boarders sometimes take to them to practice their own air moves wearing boots, boards and all. Is it a matter of time before training on the trampoline with your paddles is commonplace?

Interestingly enough, by watching videos of snowboarders, skateboarders and other freestyle 'street sports', you can see how set up and head movement combine to create pre-rotation. Watch how they set up for each spin and trick by winding up with their bodies, effectively building pre-rotation during the take off on each move, and then initiating the 'unwind' with their head movement.

Edging

The basis of many good freestyle stunts is the boater's ability to hold a kayak on edge and maintain this edge control throughout the move (bandit, cartwheel etc.).

To practice this edge control get in your boat on dry land. Lift the boat onto its edge by raising the knee opposite the balancing edge, and twisting your body so that you lean onto the uplifted knee while keeping your centre of gravity over the boat. You may have to extend your arms or paddles to help you.

After a little practice it is amazing to see how far you can get your boat on edge without toppling over. Newer, slab sided boats are particularly easy to maintain on edge for a long time.

Edge Control Exercises

Developing good edge control and awareness is fundamental to good playboating; most manoeuvres rely on the boat moving slowly relative to the hole. To do this the paddler has to stay inside the parameters of the boat but the knees, bottom and hips all need to work to change the shape of the boat in the water. Below are a couple of flat-water exercises to develop the kind of edge control you need.

On Flat Water

Place a buoy in a clear area of water.

The objective is to paddle the boat on its edge in ever decreasing circles in towards the buoy. Once at the buoy, paddle out in ever increasing circles without losing speed or control, (as if you are paddling down a 'plug hole').

At Speed

Take a 'run up to it'. Put the boat on its inside edge and paddle a wide circle, maintaining the speed. Gradually allow the back to skid out, (shifting your weight forwards in the boat helps), and control the skid with a long power stroke in the inside of the turn. Gradually shorten the power stroke from the stern and allow the circles to tighten. When the skid is at its tightest, start linking a bow draw to the front. For even tighter turns add a stern push away, creating a 'C' shaped stroke. At its tightest turn, keep the blade in the water in a continual movement, linking bow draws and stern pushes by slicing your blade through the water in a 'box' shape. You should end up with the boat spinning on its inside edge.

Edging on dry land - Paul Targett

Keep the Movement

To move back out, add a little more emphasis to the forward power part of the stroke until the slice can be removed. Then lessen the correction at the stern. The radius of the turn will increase. To increase the radius further, lessen the bow draw until only the bow power stroke remains. Gradually lengthen the stroke and bring it closer to the boat until it is a full length power stroke and bring the boat onto a straight course by using an effective stern sweep and dropping the inside edge.

When you get the hang of that, try it with the outside edge dropped. It can be done!

Different Shapes

Try paddling an 'S' shaped course with only forward paddle strokes and edges!

Trim

Dynamic trim is the trim you set into your boat during a move by leaning forwards or backwards. Dynamic trim is essential and you should 'set up the boat' to allow forward and backward movement. This will mean ensuring the back rest and knee brace are not set too high and that you have room for movement.

Inherent trim is the trim of the boat when you are sitting upright and the boat is not moving. The inherent trim of the boat should be neutral for freestyle. This is normally achieved by adjusting the seat position and footrest position. It is worth noting that, almost without exception, all manufacturers sell boats with the seat too far back, partly because it saves time in manufacture but also because it gives the impression that the boat surfs better. The trouble is to get good playboating moves you need to have a neutral trim. If you don't move your seat forwards you rapidly develop a forward lean in your paddling posture which leads to back problems and limits your performance.

Move your seat forwards!

Oscillating

At last a chance to get wet! Get in your boat on some flat water and warm up gently. Sit still in your boat and clear your mind. Capsize onto your edge. As you do this, reach forward with the drive face of your paddle on the side to which you are leaning (don't be shy, really reach). Now pull hard onto the drive face and deep into the water.

This should have the effect, if not of capsizing you, of raising the bow of the boat out of the water, slicing the stern into the water and providing enough support to maintain the edge until you have reached all the way from the bow to the stern. During this sequence it is a good idea to keep the paddles as close to the edged side of the kayak as possible, maximising the amount of power that goes into pushing the stern underwater and lifting the bow.

Photo Sequence - Tim Thomas - Hurley Weir

Top - Boat held on edge.
- The paddle is pulled back *from bow to stern* close to edged side, and bow lifts.

Middle - Bow begins to drop, boat still held on edge.
- Bow is pushed underwater by reversing pull stroke into a push from stern to bow, again blade is close to the edged side. Leaning forward will help the bow sink.

Bottom - The final pull stroke lifts the bow clear of the water, and the edged kayak rises till vertical.

Once the blade has reached from the bow to the stern there will be a slight moment of instability, as there is no power to support the edged boat. Consequently the bow will begin to drop down while still on edge. At exactly this moment, reverse the direction of the blade so that, instead of pulling on the drive face, you are pushing deep into the water with the reverse face. This should again provide enough support to maintain your edge and will push the bow into the water, fully submerging it as the stern rises.

Once this move is complete you should be back in the original edged position, with the blade near the surface at the bow. The buoyancy in the bow will start it rising. Reverse the stroke so that you are once more pulling the bow into the air, using a high brace pull stroke close to the boat. This will assist the bow in its upward travel and provide yet more support.

If your third stroke is well timed and fluid, it is possible to lift the bow up to vertical and either begin cartwheeling or back loop. Remember:

- Extend all your strokes to full reach and try to concentrate on sinking the bow deep off the second stroke.
- The deeper you sink it the more its buoyancy will assist the final loop.

Many boaters refer to this exercise as the 'double pump' and use it as the basis for many freestyle moves; eddy line cartwheels, wavewheels, even hammers.

Eddy Line Spins

Another chance to get wet (but not as wet as before). Get in your boat and find an eddy (easy so far). This is an ideal training spot for all the usual break ins and outs but also makes a good place for you to practice turning slowly on the eddy line. Eddy lines are great places to develop the subtleties of edge and blade control. Here's a couple of exercises that are great to 'play' with, whether you are new to the game or the hottest thing since the 'birdseye' chilli.

Eddy Line Spins with Sweep Strokes

Just paddle slowly onto the eddy line and allow the bow to turn into the flow; reach back with the downstream paddle and assist the flow with a strong and fluid sweep stroke from the stern.

As soon as the boat has turned, the water will catch the stern and start it turning; assist this turn with a forward sweep stroke again on the downstream paddle. Do this all the way down the eddy line. On your next go, aim to achieve more spins.

It may sound a little basic but this is another good exercise to help overcome the problem of lazy sweep strokes that hinder your freestyle progression.

Eddy Line Spins with Vertical Paddle Strokes

Approach the eddy line as above with your downstream paddle blade held vertically in the water, just behind your hip. As you cross the eddy line, slice the blade forwards across the eddy line, so that the current 'grabs' the blade. Allow the boat to be spun round, and as the stern spins into the current, slice the blade back to its original position. Immediately push against the water using the reverse face of the blade (stern pry). Once you've got the hang of this, combine bow draws and stern pries to speed up the spin. With practice you will be able to do it with the blade continually in the water.

For added realism try getting your friends to pour buckets of cold water over your head!

6 Intermediate Moves

Moves for intermediate paddlers tend to be less complex, and you only need to compare notes with the 'expert' section of this book to see that the number of different actions are usually significantly lower.

This is not to say however that intermediate moves are any easier to master than expert ones. Progression onto expert moves tends to be made by boaters who are already familiar with intermediate moves and who are developing increased spatial awareness and boat control, while intermediates are dealing with the 'newness' and lack of logic in the vertical realm. This general weirdness of flying a boat may take years to master, so don't neglect your intermediate awareness; every day spent mastering a good popout will pay dividends when you start to cartwheel. Indeed, mastery of a good 360° spin in a hole is an essential prerequisite of a good cartwheel; after all, a cartwheel is really little more than a 360° spin on a vertical axis.

Base Line Moves

Time spent doing base line moves is always beneficial to performance. The greater the variety of locations in which you can perform a manoeuvre, the more 'grooved in' it becomes. Ultimately these moves become part of a repertoire of skill that can be performed at an almost subconscious level, leaving energy and 'brain space' for more complex manoeuvres.

The Neutral Move

A concept developed for competition has been one of the 'neutral move'. Once a move becomes 'grooved in', it is possible to repeat this move as a pause in runs, but still get marks. These neutral moves are often site specific and take time to identify.

A common one is a simple front surf with carved turns. Possible on a great number of waves and better looking than a normal front surf, it scores more points and maintains movement in the run.

Flat 360s are another move often used as neutral moves. When playing a surging hole they can be used to 'buy time' while you wait until the surge is right to perform the next move in your run. Once the concept of neutral moves is understood, they need not even be visualised, they just become, as Dave Luke says, "moments of calm before the storm". (See Chapter 10.3).

6.1 Front Surfing

This move is the prerequisite to all good playboating and is a hell of a lot easier to learn than it may first appear.

We are all familiar with the concept of board surfers sticking to the wave but many non-kayakers are amazed to see boaters apparently doing the same thing on a river. The physics is of course the same, only on an ocean wave the water stays still and the wave moves forward, whereas on a river the wave stays still while the water moves forward.

Prerequisites

To perfect this move you need first to be able to paddle comfortably and with stability in a straight line, using stern rudders to correct any drift. Concentrate on paddling fluidly, with a nice rhythm and without any 'jerky' sensations.

The Move

Start by finding a wave. For your first surf it may be a good idea to choose a small one, (you aren't going to master Wimea yet), possibly on a small rapid or in small surf on the ocean. Don't, however, plump for a wave of minuscule proportions. Should you do this, the friction caused by your boat on the wave will overcome the gravity of the boat 'falling' down the wave's face and you will slip backwards off the wave, effectively dragged off the wave by physics.

On a river there are two places from where you can catch a wave, upstream of it, or from a convenient eddy. To catch your victim from above, begin by turning the boat to face upstream and dropping in on it backwards. Look over your shoulder until your stern reaches the point of contact with the wave, and begin paddling slowly, evenly, and strongly from above. Do not jerk on your paddles or bounce your body, just paddle fluidly. Three strokes should be enough to catch most waves.

From the eddy it is best to ferryglide out quite slowly. Put in a couple of strokes if necessary and relax, with a possible backwards lean as the boat drops into the trough. It is much easier to catch the wave if you start your approach close to the eddy line than if you paddle out from deep in the eddy; ideally you should almost slide onto the wave rather than force your way out of the eddy and onto it.

Once established on the wave, control the boat by leaning with your hips; further control can be gained with a few slow and strong stern rudders.

Purling

On steeper waves the bow will often purl underwater and force you to blow off the wave. Prevent this from happening by raising one of your knees, the bow will carve to the surface and you will have developed a little more spatial awareness due to 'edge control'. *Well done!*

Carving

While surfing the wave you can get used to the sensation of 'carving' and changing the direction of your surf across the wave face. To carve to the right - raise your left knee, to the left - raise your right knee. You can control the speed of your carve by using your stern rudder as a brake, pulling toward the boat as the carve picks up speed and forcing the stern further downstream. In this scenario the stern rudder should be held on the (slightly) downstream side of the boat with the blade itself held just behind your hip. Keep your arms relaxed and bent throughout the surf.

Body

During a front surf the body should be very controlled and relaxed. When catching the wave, try to avoid jerking the boat since this creates turbulence that will prohibit a good take off.

Carving on a wave, right knee lifted, boat carving to left - Matt Stephens, Skookumchuk, Canada
Photo: Pete Astles / Peak UK

Photo Sequence - Bleddyn Lloyd, Canolfan Tryweryn
Top - The kayaker leaves the eddy at a shallow angle and 'sliiiidess' onto the wave.
Bottom - Establishing himself in a surf with a slight forward lean.
   - Never look at the camera!

Keep your weight slightly forwards during the take off and lean gently back only when fully established on the wave.

Coach's Top Tip

I often watch freestyle paddlers try to make up in brute force what they lack in finesse. Take the time to 'read' the water. Waves are subtle. Most waves are chevron shaped, and the best place to get on them from the eddy is where the wave begins to take shape on the outside of the chevron. This spot is often upstream of the steepest part of the wave.

Now relax. You've got it sussed. Approach it gently. Don't try and 'mug' the wave. The trick is to sneak up on it and, 'pick its pocket'.

Franco Ferrero is head of the canoesport department at Plas y Brenin, the UK National Mountain Centre, and is sponsored by Palm and Pyranha.

Your well padded boat should be easy to control by tilting the hips gently; a right hand tilt will cause the boat to carve (rather than turn) to the right. Don't over tilt or tilt crazily from edge to edge, at best you will look a prat, at worst...*Ouch!*

Coaching Points:

1. Remember that the amount of edge and/or body lean you use will depend on the speed of the boat and wave.
2. Access to the wave is best achieved by ferry gliding through the lowest point of the wave, i.e. across the trough of the wave.
3. You should be aiming to complete the manoeuvre out onto the wave without a build up of water on or around the bow of the boat.

Boat

During take off, the hull of the boat should stay flush with the water and cruise smoothly as the boater paddles. This is easy to do when dropping onto the wave from upstream, but slightly more difficult when ferrygliding out from the eddy as the bow tends to hit the green water first and swing downstream. By carefully choosing to catch the wave from close to the eddy line you should be able to overcome this problem and slide smoothly onto the wave (ferry-*glide!*).

When the boat first catches the wave it will want to drop all the way down to the trough. Control this with slight body leans forwards (to speed up) and backwards (to slow down). If necessary, try sharp dabbing reverse paddle strokes; they will pull the boat up the wave.

The bow is controlled by the boat's carving action across the wave face, and any 'purling' is countered by edging the boat.

Blades

When catching the wave, paddle strokes should be strong, smooth and have rhythm; two or three good strokes should be enough to catch the wave.

Steering

The blades and paddles can provide the additional purchase needed to initiate the turn. As you place the blade close to the stern in a rudder position, steering can be achieved by pushing the blade away from the stern and imagining you are sliding your bum along a bench. Care has to be taken to avoid pushing the blade beyond 15° from the keel line, as it then acts as a brake and will drag you up and off the wave. If you've forgotten your protractor you can take another approach. Set up the stern rudder as before but, rather than pushing the blade away to create the turn, gently roll your wrists away from the boat and lift your front arm. This pushes the angled blade deep into the wave and gives you the turn.

Common Mistakes

Too much jerking prohibits a good surf and might just make you blind! It is a symptom of 'wanting the wave too much', and can only be overcome with a more relaxed attitude and by developing a strong and fluid paddling style.

Purling sometimes cannot be helped but can in most instances be controlled with a gradual raise of the upstream knee. Generally, during a surf run one knee will be slightly upstream of the other. This is because all river features have a degree of 'kick', and most boaters offset this kick by holding the boat at an angle during a surf. The buoyancy in the boat will have less water piling down onto it and will soon rise to the surface. Should you experiment and slightly raise the downstream knee, considerable amounts of water will pile onto the deck of your boat; some of this water will build up against the upstream edge and you may dynamically flip upstream... you have been warned!

Feeling the Wave

Developing a 'feel' for surfing is often the most difficult thing. You'll recognise it when you've done it but it is such a 'feely' kinesthetic thing that just talking about it or watching someone is not enough. A good way to get into surfing is this zig-zag exercise on a series of standing waves.

From the eddy on one side, 'ferry' across the wave into the opposite eddy. The key principle is to move onto the wave at its lowest point (in the trough).

Continue to try the cross, gradually reducing the strokes required until it can be achieved with no paddle strokes on the wave; use a stern rudder on the upstream side as you cross the wave and lots of upstream edge. Surf/high cross into the eddy line and, as you cross onto the eddy line, raise the front hand and look back towards the wave. Visualise sliding your bottom away from the paddle.

The boat will turn and also move slightly downstream. A good power stroke on the opposite side to the stern rudder should push you back onto the second wave. The stroke is held at the stern to act as a stern rudder on the second cross. This can be repeated onto the third and then the fourth wave.

If you have difficulty at first, use more power strokes to regain the wave, but aim to get the turn closer to the wave each time by reducing the strokes needed to get back on to the wave, and starting the sequence on the eddy line, or even whilst still on the wave.

6.2 Hole Riding

Having mastered the front surf, many intermediates will want to familiarise themselves with stopper sitting, sometimes called side surfing. Unfortunately, the broken and chaotic nature of a hole is often enough to put first timers off. Even more experienced river boaters find coming to terms with *wanting* to be in the hole a massive obstacle to progressing at freestyle.

Prerequisites

Since only more confident kayakers will want to play in holes, we'll leave the basics of forward paddling and stern rudders alone. Essentially all you really need to ride a hole is an ability to hold a boat on edge, confidence and a good set of low and (God forbid) high brace support strokes.

If you are not confident with any of these then best leave alone for a while. Go to a pool or calm river and chuck yourself around, practising sculling and supports. Try improving your edge control through a dry land exercise as illustrated in Chapter 5.

The Move

Begin by finding your wave. This should be relatively easy to do since most of the safe and accessible ones in Britain are usually surrounded by half man, half fish creatures dressed in lurid colours (other kayakers). (See Chapter 2 for features of a 'good' hole).

Now is a good time to try a visualisation exercise while you work up courage. Watch the other boaters and what they are doing in the hole; concentrate on what they are doing right rather than what they are doing wrong.

Your turn in the hole will come later than you think, since in any collection of kayakers there are always one or two who seem to think they have a divine right to push in. Just move up the eddy queue and sit near the hole. Most playboaters will let you go first since your nervous looks will give you away as someone who is not likely to be in the hole long, and you are likely to make them look good by comparison!

Ferry gliding into the hole is a frequent stumbling block. Concentrate on keeping your boat angled, not drifting downstream, and staying calm. Never flail your way into the hole! It is handy to try and catch the hole as you would catch a wave during a front surf from an eddy. Try and start quite close to the eddy line and 'slide' onto the hole, rather than paddling out from deep in the eddy and catching too much water on your bow as it enters the green water.

As you drop into the hole, the water will naturally push your bow around so that you are facing across the hole. Smoothly edge your boat and low brace onto the hole's pile; the low brace should really only take a very small amount of pressure and you should keep your centre of gravity balanced over the boat. With practice you may even lift your paddles away from the pile and remain comfortably side surfing the hole.

Too much edge during a side surf and you will pull yourself up and out of the hole, too little and you will dynamically power flip upstream. If this happens *do not* try to support yourself with an upstream brace, just tuck your body up and let the boat flip. You should easily roll up on the downstream side of the boat.

When sitting in the hole, both your arms should be relaxed and slightly bent so as to absorb any shocks or sudden bounces the hole may produce.

To move in the hole, a combination of forward and backward body leans and forward and backward paddle strokes should help. To move forward - lean towards the bow and pull on the drive face of the supporting paddle, to reverse - lean slightly back and push on the blade's reverse face. Be careful here not to lean back too much, as this will only unsettle you. Your body talk during a hole ride should be very subtle, and your body should lean slightly forward most of the time.

Side surfing a hole - Darryl Sergisson, Holme Pierpont

Body

A relaxed stance will work best, it's really not as scary as it might appear at first. When in the hole, concentrate on raising the upstream knee, edging the boat just enough and using your hips and arms to absorb any bounces. Keep your body weight over the boat as you did during the edging exercise, rather than leaning onto the hole's pile. By leaning slightly forward during a hole ride you will keep your centre of gravity lower, while at the same time be able to tuck quickly should you flip upstream.

Flipping in the hole requires split second timing to avoid a potentially injurious event. Tuck your body and blades forward and roll on the downstream side.

Slight body leans, forward and back, will help move the boat across the hole and may assist when manoeuvring for an exit.

Powerflip - Mind those edges!

Boat

Edge control is the key to mastery of hole riding. Just enough edge during the ferry glide will get you in the hole, too much or too little and you will either break in too sharply and miss the hole or flip upstream and look really dumb.

Carve the boat using your hips as you enter the hole, so you don't plunge into the maw and inadvertently front loop.

Once sitting in the hole, your boat should be edged with all upstream edges slightly raised above the ramp of water. A little more than two inches is a reasonable margin of safety and will allow a comfortable side surf. Too much edge will cause you to be unstable in the hole and will look and feel awkward. Choose a forgiving hole and experiment!

Blades

Stern rudders should control your entry into the hole, and the downstream blade hardly need leave the water to transfer to a low brace support once the hole has been entered. It is best to scull in most holes on a low brace and keep your arms relaxed and slightly bent; we wouldn't want to dislocate those shoulders now would we! If you are edging the boat correctly during a side surf, you need hardly put any pressure at all on the support blade, and may even lift them out of the water while maintaining a side surf (very cool).

Common Mistakes

1. Flipping upstream. Reread all the warnings about edge control and do a few exercises to make sure it is up to scratch. Then go back to a hole with a less steep ramp and practice a little more.
2. Bouncing in the hole. This is caused by bad body talk; further practice of the edging exercises in this section will again overcome this problem.

Coaching Points

The first thing required in good hole work is edge control. The ideal is to be able to sit in a hole without any weight on the paddle. This is achieved by combining knee lift on the upstream side and putting weight over the downstream bottom cheek. This is often assisted by looking downstream.

Three good exercises and tips that can help with this are:

1. If you discover that every time you get into a hole, your paddle sinks beneath the water surface closely followed by you; this is caused by leaning downstream. As you get into the stopper imagine the work being done by your knee and paddle. On a scale of 1-10 you should have 1 for the paddle and perhaps a 7 for the knee. Experiment to achieve the balance, in both senses.
2. When you enter the hole, do you find you get tired rapidly and then disappear gently beneath the wave, sculling or bracing for support? People often learn to support by leaning back on the stern deck of the boat. This actually prevents you from using your hips effectively, so try to sit up. Your centre of gravity is now higher, but then again you shouldn't have your centre of gravity outside the boat, so it's not an issue.
3. If you are still encountering a couple of problems, try entering the hole with some speed and maintaining this as you move along it. This accommodates any lean you may still have and ensures that you lessen your dependence on the blade, as its role has changed from supporting to providing power.

6.3 Hole Spinning

Simply sitting in a hole soon becomes a little tedious, and you know when you are ready to advance when your friends begin shouting, "Do something", from the eddy. Fortunately it is quite simple to progress onto more advanced moves and silence your doubters. Spinning in the hole means a flat, rather than vertical, spin on the edge of the hole where the green water rushes past it, and is often referred to as a flat spin. Most of the work is done by the water as the green water pushes one end of the boat out of the hole and the towback pulls the other end into the hole.

Prerequisites

Before attempting this move you should have a number of things wired. The most important of these are sitting in a hole comfortably and edge control. Combine these with strong support strokes and the ability to transfer edges and you are sorted.

Transferring edges simply means changing the side on which you are edging the boat as the boat spins round, so that the upstream edge is always held clear of the hole's ramp. It is sometimes known as a 'transition'. The transition needs to be achieved smoothly and at the same speed as the spin. Fast holes require snappy transitions, slow holes slow ones. This can be practised on flat water using visualisation techniques.

The Move

Get steady sitting in the hole; you should be on a nice low brace and very relaxed. Let's assume you are going to start the spin on the bow. Lean forward and put in a positive forward stroke to push the boat to the side of the hole.

As the boat starts to turn, kill the forward stroke and put a little backward pressure on the support blade. This should have the effect of stopping the forward drift and preventing the boat from leaving the hole altogether. The bow will catch the water flowing downstream at the edge of the hole (the 'green water'). Allow the green water to turn your bow downstream but keep your brace firm on the pile.

Photo Sequence - Steve Whetman - Photos: Helen Metcalfe / Nookie

Above - Kayaker holds boat on edge in a stable side surf.
- Centre of gravity is *over* the edged boat.

Top Right - Paddler eases the boat to the 'sweet spot', bow begins to turn downstream.
- Edge is maintained and the brace continues as the bow sweeps around.

Middle Right - Edge and brace are switched *smoothly* to the opposite edge.
- Back push on the low brace stroke helps to push boat back into the hole.
- Stern begins to spin downstream.

Bottom Right - Another 'transition' (change of edge) and smooth forward stroke, and the boat drops back into the hole, ending up in the original side surf position.

This is probably the hardest part of the move, since as soon as the bow is pointing downstream, you should transfer your edge to the opposite side and with it your low brace. At the same time you should put in a hard reverse stroke to push your stern back into the hole.

The hole's 'sweet spot' is the best spot in the hole for your chosen move. In a flat spin it's usually at the hole's side, or where a chute pushes through the hole breaking it into two separate holes. If you are sitting in the sweet spot, the stern should catch the green water almost immediately and will begin to turn. The green water effectively 'swings' the stern round to point downstream. As soon as you are facing upstream, swap edges and drop back into the hole with a forward stroke on the downstream side of the boat.

If, when facing downstream, you have dropped back into the hole and 'stalled' away from the sweet spot, use your low brace to push you back towards sweetness until the end of the boat catches. As soon as you are facing upstream, a positive forward stroke will push you back to the sweet spot.

Body

To initiate the move from a side surf, a forward lean helps to push the boat towards the side of the hole. Many boaters maintain this forward lean throughout the move and are thus well protected should the unthinkable happen and they flip upstream.

Edge control is all important throughout the move and edges should be transferred using the hips and knees. Remember to keep your centre of gravity over the boat.

Another important thing to think of is where to look. If you get this sorted it will make the vertical plane easier to deal with. Good practice is to keep your eyes fixed over the boat and into the hole as long as possible. Don't be shy of looking over your upstream shoulder. As soon as you change edges and blade, snap your head around to look back into the hole. This whole 'looking' thing looks very neat when done well, and disgustingly sloppy when done badly. You will know when you have got it wired, it just feels right and looks considerably smoother.

Boat

When sitting in a hole never overedge your boat. This encourages high brace supports and allows the boat to bounce in the hole.

As the bow starts to turn at the hole's edge, maintain your edge and reduce the degree of 'edge' slightly as the boat starts to point downstream. Once it faces downstream, the edge of the boat is changed smoothly and the boat is eased back into the hole, stern first. This edge is maintained as the stern turns, and only transferred once the boat is facing upstream. From this point the boat drops forward, back into the sweet spot.

Blades

Low brace! Then use the drive face to ease the boat's bow out of the hole, don't be afraid to control the amount of bow 'caught' by the green water with reverse strokes as your feet cross the sweet spot.

Continue the low brace support until the boat is facing downstream and then swap blades to support on. As you do this, a reverse stroke on the new blade will push the boat backwards. As the boat faces upstream, another blade swap is called for, and a sharp forward stroke will begin the spin again.

Common Mistakes

By far the most common mistake for newcomers is trying too hard for the move, allowing the boat to accelerate towards the sweet spot and past it out of the hole. Counter this by holding the boat in a static position in the hole as you enter it, as though you are just going to sit in the hole. Then ease *slowly* to the edge of the hole using calm forward and reverse strokes to limit the amount of 'catch' (the amount of green water caught by the bow).

A more dangerous mistake is catching the edges of your boat and flipping upstream. This can actually appear like a more advanced move called a bandit when the landing is upright and in control. When out of control and unintentional, it can smart a little and may leave the exposed shoulders vulnerable to dislocation. It is usually caused by the boater changing edges too soon, and can be countered by watching the boat turn while looking back into the hole as long as possible. By looking over your shoulder, you should be able to see where your boat's edges will catch in the maw and where they will not, thus saving you a good old 'trashing'.

Coaching Point

Some principles are common throughout kayaking and one of them is: the easiest way to turn a boat is to ensure that the ends of the boat are out of the water as you turn. To do this your flat spins will need to happen at the top of the pile, i.e. you on top of the mound of water.

A good exercise is to imagine a series of waves as moguls on a ski run. Passively float down the waves. Do this a couple of times, eyes shut, eyes open, facing upstream, facing downstream and across the current.

Once confident at that site, try to turn the boat on the top of the waves on one run and then in the troughs on the second.

Take several runs. The point should be illustrated that easier turns happen when the boat is on the crest of the waves whilst the ends are 'free', as opposed to in the trough of the waves when the bow and stern are trapped by the wave upstream and downstream.

Once demonstrated try to turn 360° in three waves, then two, then on one.

Or try turning the boat to face one bank then the other, flick flack, with wide strokes to act as turn and positioning strokes. Finally, go back to the hole and time your turn so that it happens on top of the pile.

6.4 Popouts

By now you will probably be eager to get vertical and finish your already impressive run with an aerial move. Of all the air moves the popout is the most basic but requires a good level of skill to master and stay controlled. The basic physics of the popout are very similar to the physics behind a cork under pressure. Take a cork with you to the bath and push it underwater; the inherent buoyancy in the cork will push the cork up and sometimes out of the water - popout!

Prerequisites

Probably the most important of all the prerequisites to a popout is selecting your spot. In Britain many holes are shallow, and any attempt to popout will result in a clumsy and often damaging experience. Find a hole that is not only deep enough but has enough water flowing over it to push your bow downwards.

A popout can often be done on a wave by allowing your boat to 'purl' during a front surf on a wave. The principles of popping out on waves and in holes are broadly similar and, having mastered the pop out on one, you will find it quite easy to transfer this skill onto other water features.

The next prerequisite is a good roll. It is amazing how many boaters can pull a good 'endo' but flail like kippers when it comes to recovery time, or others who will 'kill' the move by spinning 180° in an attempt to avoid capsizing.

Finally, it is important to hold the boat straight onto the downstream flow, allowing the bow to purl straight into the green water. In modern freestyle boats this is actually quite difficult, since the low volume ends of such kayaks are designed to slice through the water and often slip sideways during a popout.

The Move

In a good popout, the bow of the boat is introduced with control straight into the 'green' water flowing under a hole or wave. The green water pushes the bow downstream while the wave or hole itself acts as a pivot. As the boat gets vertical, the inherent buoyancy in the bow will push the boat upwards and the boat may even leave the water, 'popping out' and into the air.

In order to get a good popout the boater must be comfortable surfing the boat with the bow pointing upstream. The bow of the boat will often 'purl' under the water as soon as the boater ceases to edge the boat. Encourage this purling with an aggressive forward body lean and the bow should catch enough green water to initiate the move.

It is important to prevent the boat from slipping out sideways from under you during the initial 'catch'. A good stern rudder usually helps this and can be maintained until the boat reaches vertical.

Once the boat is vertical the blades are by and large redundant unless you are trying for a more advanced variation on the move. A continuation of the forward lean will help you 'loop' forward for an upside down landing, while a sudden lean back, standing on the boat's footrest, will initiate some good 'air time' and probably (although not definitely), an upright landing.

Body

To initiate a popout, the body will control the boat through carving during the surf using the hips and knees. Kill the carve and allow the bow to 'catch' by dropping down the wave face so that the bow digs into the wave or hole's ramp. As soon as the bow begins to purl underwater, lean aggressively forward and encourage the boat's bow further underwater.

As the bow plunges underwater, keep the boat stable using your hips; any edge will allow the boat to slip to the side. Maintain the forward lean until you are near vertical and decide on your choice: lean back and higher 'air' may be gained and an upright landing is probable, lean forward for a loop and an upside down landing.

Boat

Boat control during a popout is imperative. If it is your first attempt you should concentrate on introducing the bow in a slow and controlled manner. Keep the whole of the bow flush with the green water, so as to catch as much of the downstream flow as possible. This usually means keeping the bow facing upstream, although in more 'squirrelly' water slight edge may be required. A good example of this is when trying to popout on the downstream side of a mid river rock where the residue from the cushion spills around the side of the rock.

Blades

To initiate the move the blades should control the speed with which the bow enters the green water. A few dabbing reverse strokes will slow the boat as it drops down the hole or wave and a stern rudder while the bow catches will prevent slipping and keep the boat straight.

Once airborne the blades are almost useless since they are not in contact with the water. Throw them away or spin them for extra brownie points, but remember that you may need them to roll.

Common Mistakes

The most common mistake in shallow sites is allowing the boat to enter the hole too fast. In pourovers you will likely collide with the rock forming the pourover. *Slow down*, control is more graceful than power.

Those new to the vertical plane will often 'kill' the move almost as soon as it has begun. They enter the hole with a dynamic forward lean and lean back as soon as the bow has caught, countering the plunge of the bow. Keep the forward lean as long as possible while you get used to the idea of flying, and accept the odd forced roll as part and parcel of your learning curve.

Allowing the boat to slip sideways under you will result in a clumsy popout at best and a good 'trashing' at worst. Keep controlled with a stern rudder and minimal edge, and slow down. Concentrate on getting the sensation of standing on your footrest.

Photo Sequence – James Shrimpton – Canolfan Tryweryn

Top Left – Paddler *looks* exactly at the point where he is planting the bow.
- Paddles control the speed of entry into the downstream flow (the 'green water').

Bottom Left – Bow begins to 'purl' underwater as green water piles onto the deck.
- Slight forward lean encourages the bow's 'purl'.

Above – Bow plunges completely down.
- Paddles become almost redundant at this point.
- The paddler must now lean back and stand on the footrest to prevent the stern 'looping over'.

6.5 Back Loops

Although you may have pulled this move off countless times on a river (remember, immediately preceding that working-over you had), it is quite a difficult move to pull off with finesse. Essentially, a reverse loop is the same as a popout, with one notable exception: instead of initiating on the bow you allow the stern to catch and the bow to flip over your head. Sounds complicated... It isn't!

Prerequisites

A 'go for it' attitude and an ability to roll, not much else.

The Move

In a pourover many boaters will pull this move off by simply paddling backwards up to the fall, allowing the stern to catch, and hanging on until it all goes calm. In a hole the same principle applies although it is sometimes quite difficult to manoeuvre the boat so that it's facing downstream. Go back to your flat spins in a hole and initiate the move by not transferring edges as the stern drops back into the hole.

Since many modern playboats have short flat backs they tend to shed water quite slowly and so back loops are often quicker than their forward cousins. Remember to reverse into the hole slowly and in control. Don't edge the boat since this will probably result in a reverse break-in (eddy-out) and possibly an unplanned hole ride.

When going for a simple back loop, don't be tempted to look over your shoulder once the stern has caught. The pre-rotation from your body which will result from such a glance will allow the boat to slip and may help you retain the hole, something which experts like but intermediates may find disconcerting.

Body

While reversing into the hole or spinning the boat into position, look over your shoulder at the stern. You will then be able to predict when the stern catches and respond accordingly. As soon as the stern begins to catch, look forward, this will kill any pre-rotation you have built up and allow a cleaner back loop.

Concentrate on *not* edging the boat, and allowing the whole of the stern to catch the green water flush. Just sit in your boat and wait for it. Leaning back as the stern catches will undoubtedly help initiate the move but a forward lean once the stern has caught will probably have a negligible effect. Nearly all back loops end in a capsize, hence the name (rather than reverse popout).

Boat

Ease the stern slowly into the green water and allow it to catch fully by having no edge. This should prevent the boat from slipping out. As soon as the stern has caught, hang on! The back loop tends to happen very quickly.

Blades

Only useful here for initiating the move and controlling the speed of the boat. As soon as the stern has caught it is a good idea to move your blades into roll position. This should protect you if you end up back in the hole, and save time setting up once the move is over.

Common Mistakes

I have never seen anyone trying this move fail, it's that simple. If you do have problems, take a look at how you are entering the hole. The problem will usually lie in the initiation, so practice your flat spins and/or back paddling.

6.6 Tail Squirts and Variations

Kayaking on the vertical plane is more than a little addictive, and once getting ends in a hole has been mastered, many boaters will want to advance to verticality on eddy lines. In a sense finding a place to practice tail squirts is really easy; while safe playholes are infrequently encountered, nearly every section of flowing water has an eddy line strong and deep enough to allow this move to be practised.

Note: Cartwheels are often counted in terms of the number of 'ends'; that is the number of times each end of the boat rises in an arc.

Prerequisites

Had I been writing this book a few years ago I'm sure this move would have counted as 'expert', but learnt correctly this is a very easy move, especially in a modern low volume playboat with its sharp edges and flat decks. Start building towards it by practising your sweep strokes, they really need to be strong and confident in order to tail squirt well. Then start thinking about 'charc'; although mystified by squirt devotees, charc is just a clever word for 'changing arc'.

To understand this concept try breaking in and out of the flow a few times (as in the eddy spinning exercises earlier in this section). Easy isn't it? Once you have done a few break-ins, vary the angle with which you approach the eddy. By doing so you have altered your 'charc' and you will require a slightly different degree of edge to break in smoothly.

To summarise, a good tail squirt needs strong sweep strokes, 'charc' and a degree of edge control.

The Move

Let's start by assuming that you are going to tail squirt as you leave an eddy and enter the flowing water. Contrary to popular belief, this move does not happen best in the green water, but on the eddy line where the water tends to be slightly more confused and frothy. Look for indicators of a good eddy line such as small whirlpools, swirls and bubbles; where these appear is the optimum place for your tail squirts.

Since this move is best done in a controlled rather than a forced way, practice doing it slowly at first. A mistake many newcomers make is to paddle hell for leather at the eddy line and rush the move.

As your bow leaves the eddy it will naturally begin to turn downstream; this usually happens as your feet cross the eddy line. Allow the boat to turn and assist the turn with a strong forward sweep on the upstream side of the boat. Once the boat has turned to face almost downstream, change your blades to the opposite side of the boat and reach far back with the paddle for a strong sweep stroke from the stern of the boat. Don't be shy, *really* reach. Remember to protect yourself from injury by keeping this arm slightly bent.

As you change blades transfer your edge from the conventional downstream edge to a slight upstream edge. Practice this a few times without going for the tail squirt. You should feel water build up on the boat's stern and a little bit of fizzing as it does so *but,* there should be insufficient pressure on your stern to capsize you.

Once you are familiar with the sensation of an upstream lean on leaving the eddy, it is time to *go for it*! This time as soon as you transfer the edge, begin a strong positive sweep stroke from the stern. The pressure should be on the reverse face of the blade; if you have sufficient edge, this single stroke will be enough to drive the stern deeper into the water and lift the bow up. Hold the sweep as long as possible and you should be able to lift the bow clear of the water and up to (or past) vertical. Congratulations! You can now taily.

Having pushed your boat into a vertical position, it is sometimes possible to stay vertical, spinning down the eddy line on the boat's tail. To do this, change blades and put in a sort of vertical draw stroke on the opposite side of the boat, this draw stroke should catch quite a lot of green water and pull the boat into a vertical spin, very cool!

Performer's Top Tip

The changing arc; the change of direction in which you are travelling. The idea is that you set up a charc going into a move, and that charc carries on all the way through the move. Basically it's all a linked concept with 'future water' and 'future moves'; you plan a charc going into a move and it follows through all the way to the end.

For example: Going into a stern squirt from leaving the eddy, paddle in a straight line and set up with a sweep stroke just before you hit the eddy line so you're travelling in an arc going towards the eddy line. Hit the eddy line at exactly 90° and that's when you initiate the tail with a hip move down into the flow. When your boat aligns with the current is when you hit vertical.

Andy 'Snakey' Whiting was joint Silver Medalist in the Squirt Boat class at the 1997 Ottawa Freestyle Worlds. He is supported by Peak UK and Riot.

Body

As the legs cross the eddy line and the boat begins to turn, accentuate the forward sweep stroke to assist the boat's turn (charc). I've mentioned this in the body section since you need to really reach and that requires extra body torque.

As soon as the forward stroke is over, *really* reach back downstream for a positive stern sweep. At the same time look over the upstream shoulder. This will increase the degree of pre-rotation and help force the stern underwater. As you begin the sweep, switch your edges by raising the downstream knee and tilting your hips upstream slightly. Remember it is only the hips that tilt the boat upstream. Just like during a side surf your actual body weight should remain *over* the kayak. *Do not* tilt your body weight upstream.

Boat

Edge control is all important in this move, too little and the boat will hardly rise, too much and you will flip upstream, so go out and practice.

As your legs cross the eddy line you will typically be edging downstream as in a break-in. As soon as the boat begins to turn, transfer to an upstream edge (not too much) and maintain this edge until the stern is forced underwater. With a strong stern sweep the boat may continue to spin balanced on its tail along the eddy line.

Performer's Top Tip

Screwing around... The trick with these moves is to know how far past vertical you can go without overbalancing and face planting into the water. The solution to this lies in plenty of practice... keep the boat spinning to present the tail flat to the direction in which you are falling; the imaginary fall line... As soon as you turn the boat sideways, the tail will slash upwards and the bow will fall. Whereas if you keep the tail flat the boat will fall quite slowly. Key elements of a tail squirt are a little bit of weight throw, reaching around the boat to 'future water' with the paddle, and knowing when you can't go any further because you've run out of reach... Then you know you have to bring the boat down on its hull and finish the move, but by then you've been screwing around so long everyone thinks you're a star!

Bill Mattos, as well as being a top British rodeo star, is owner of Nookie paddlewear manufacturers and leader of Nookie's infamous Team Extreme.

Blades

Start by paddling forwards as in a break-in (eddy-out). As your feet cross the eddy line, help the boat's turn with a fluid forward sweep on the upstream side. As soon as this sweep loses power (as the blade moves towards the stern), switch blades and put in a strong backwards sweep on the opposite side of the boat.

Strong positive strokes are the key to this move. You can practice the required degree of stroke through bench spinning and spinning on eddy lines.

Common Mistakes

Too much edge will cause you to capsize. You can tell when this happens because you will feel as though you are tripping over your upstream edge and your head will get wet! Best way to resolve this problem is to practice the move a few times, particularly the initiation, without going for the full taily.

Too little edge will barely raise the bow, the same practice exercise should resolve this problem.

Going for it too fast; many people trying their first few tail squirts seem to mistake it for a power move rather than the graceful and controlled move it really is. These are also the same people who tend to trip over their upstream edge. Just slow down and relax; kayaking is a cool and relaxed sport, not an exercise in doing damage to your body.

Coaching points

The taily is a very subtle technique that is hard to do because it simply goes against the grain of what we do to break-in. We apparently have to lean upstream to do it; as we all know, leaning upstream doesn't get a taily, it just gets us wet! Like most play boating techniques this is subtle, requiring balance and timing.

"Think BAT - Balance, Accuracy, Timing" - Ray Rowe, BCU Level 5 Coach.

Set yourself up as if performing a break-in (eddy out). Approach the break-in in the same way but as you cross the eddy line, at the point you would normally raise your upstream knee, don't! This time push against the footrest with that leg instead. This will drop the knee from the brace and create a very subtle upstream edge. Keep your weight inside the boat. This has to be combined with a good reverse sweep stroke, and the analogy of pushing your bum away from the paddle works well here. This will drive the stern underwater and into the current, causing the bow to rise.

Still having a hard time? Does your reverse stroke seem to come out of the water and the taily never seem to come vertical? We are so used to working in one plane that as we do the reverse sweep, we do not anticipate the bow rising, so we literally reverse sweep the paddle out of the water. To correct it, as you sweep, sweep both towards the bow but also diagonally down into the water. This will keep the blade on the surface as the bow rises.

You seem to get vertical but you can't sustain it and you've come to the end of your sweep? Next time modify your reverse sweep. This stroke starts from the rear of the kayak, twist round so you can reach the stern of the boat with your paddle. Keep your arm straight and sweep the paddle out and down and towards the bow of the boat; the blade needs to stay just under the surface. As the blade comes parallel to your hip, twist the paddle so your wrists drop below the paddle shaft. This will twist the blade so the drive face now faces the bow. Now continue the draw towards the bow. This front portion of the stroke is rather ineffective unless your top hand is raised gradually, so that by the time the blade reaches the boat you are dangling the paddle from your top hand. A simple feather of the blade so it can be sliced away form the bow, and the draw repeated, will enable you to keep the rotation needed to keep the stern driving into the water.

Variations

The really great thing about tail squirts is the amount of variations you can try, in order to get the same effect.

Cut Backs

Instead of initiating the move on a break-in, enter the green water at a shallower angle. Push the bow of the boat towards the eddy with a strong forward sweep on the downstream side and edge the boat upstream. Then transfer your blade and sweep backwards on the blade that is now closest to the eddy. This will have the effect of tail squirting the boat on the opposite edge to the conventional tail squirt, and can sometimes allow you to hang the boat in the air longer, almost 'splatting' the eddy line that borders the eddy.

High Brace Tailies

Once you are happy tail squirting on a reverse sweep, try squirting the stern down on the original forward sweep; this tends to be faster since you need not lose seconds transferring your blades. When tail squirting off this high brace stroke, increase the amount of upstream edge slightly, and concentrate on pushing down with the high brace more than around, as you would with a sweep stroke.

Marcel Marceau

A move practised out of sheer boredom and discovered quite by accident. Paddle backwards out of the eddy straight into the flow. As soon as the stern starts to turn, edge the boat upstream and support on an upstream high brace. Timed right, the bow will be forced upwards and you should be able to hold it vertical quite a long time since all the turning momentum has been killed.

Photo Sequence - Bill Mattos - Photos: Helen Metcalfe / Nookie

Left - Paddler leaves eddy with slight forward speed.
- Note that the paddler here is looking at the point where he intends to tail squirt.

Middle - The paddler's knees cross the eddy line.
- As the bow sweeps downstream the boater edges slightly upstream.
- Paddler reaches back to initiate a strong sweep stroke from the downstream side.
- Note that although the boat is edged upstream the paddler's body weight remains over the centre line of the kayak.

Right - The sweep from the stern is maintained until the bow raises to vertical.

6.7 Screw Ups

Although this is as much a river survival technique as a freestyle move in its own right, it is a handy tactic to have in your repertoire. In essence, a screw up is an Eskimo roll performed very early as the boat stands on its stern following a back loop or, more commonly, a tail squirt.

Prerequisites

One of the main prerequisites to a screw up is the ability to get into a situation where you need to do it (a tail squirt or bandit). Combine this with a good strong Eskimo roll and you should have it sorted in minutes.

The Move

One of the great things about tail squirting is that the rotation built up during the move can be maintained, with practice, so that the boat spins on its stern along the chosen eddy line. This rotation can be used so that, even as the boat goes past vertical and back loops over, a quick screw up ensures an upright landing and you hardly get your hair wet.

The move is quite simple. As the boat goes past vertical on the stern and the bow begins to drop (so that you would normally land upside down), reach up and across toward the

Photo Sequence – Jim Shrimpton, Canolfan Tryweryn
Top - As the boat tips just past vertical the paddler has reached back and around, keeping the blade on the surface.
    - By pushing down on this blade he maintains the boat's rotation and initiates the screw up.
Middle - Pressure is maintained on the screw up blade throughout the move so that the boat lands upright.
Bottom - Upright again!
    - Note that the paddler comes out of the screw up in forward paddling posture, ready to begin the next move immediately or, on a river, to set up to punch the next meaty hole!

direction of spin, as you would when setting up for a screw roll, and plant the blade's drive face cleanly on the surface of the water. In a tail squirt this is usually done with the paddle that initiated the tail squirt, the low brace stern sweep blade. Downward pressure on this blade will start a very early, past vertical Eskimo roll, and if you reach around with your body in the same direction and lean hard forward, the boat will rotate another 180°, landing you upright on the eddy line.

The possibilities with this move are endless: avoiding trashings in nasty holes by screwing up and out of them, spinning out of a hole on the tail as an exit move in competition, or simply screwing up quickly from a variety of freestyle moves to retain the wave and extend your run.

Body

Remember that it is handy to have built up a little pre-rotation and that your boat should at least be slightly rotating on the stern. This rotation can be aided by twisting your body trunk around the side of the boat on which you intend to screw up. Reach across and around with your arms and *lean forward*. (This should help to slow the back loop and give you more control during the move).

As the boat falls off the vertical, *look* over the shoulder nearest the twisting edge. This will encourage the boat to land where you are looking. It will also give you a possibly essential millisecond to respond, if you see that type of thing you *really* don't want to be landing on!

Boat

Imagine that the boat is standing vertical on its stern and rotating slightly. This is because of the power of the paddle stroke that forced it onto its stern, combined with the body rotation built up during the move.

It is sometimes possible to maintain this taily for an extended period and rotate the boat two or even three times, as though the boat is pirouetting on its stern along the eddy line (or even better out of a stopper). Usually however, the boat's bow will go past vertical and start to fall upside down on top of the boater. By screwing up, instead of landing upside down, the boat will continue to spin as the bow falls, and you will land upright and smiling on the eddy line.

Blade

As the bow rises to vertical, initiate the boat's spin by putting a vertical draw stroke on the side in which you wish to spin. It sounds difficult, but by leaning forward and drawing the drive face of the blade toward you, the spin can often be rapid and even enough to land you upright on its own.

As soon as the boat goes vertical, reach around with the opposite blade as far as you can and push downwards, just as you would in a conventional screw roll. With timing the screw up will feel natural and surprisingly easy. After all, it's really only a screw roll performed early.

Common Mistakes

Mistiming this move will simply result in a back loop. Re-set up and roll, then head to your taily or ender spot and have another try!

6.8 Splats

This is one of the most dangerous moves in the playboater's repertoire. Done well it provides little or no danger to the boater. If mistimed, or done on a badly selected rock, a simple splat can turn from a fun game into a major river incident and a difficult to extract pin. For this reason I will first dwell on where and what to splat.

What to Splat

A simple rule of thumb is never to splat anything that may have been in the river for less than five thousand years. This particularly refers to trees since they tend to have nasty things called branches which can punch a neat hole in your expensive equipment or even snag you and seriously spoil your day. This five thousand year rule is equally applicable to rafts and other boaters, particularly when they are not expecting it. Rafters who have been splatted often end with a kayak underneath them and have been known to order their clients to stamp their feet as the kayak passes underneath as revenge; fair game.

By far the best thing to splat is a smooth rock with a decent cushion wave on the upstream face. *Be careful.* A cushion wave is no guarantee that the rock is not undercut, so check out your chosen rock carefully. A good way of doing this is to trick a paddling buddy into going first, but this will not win their respect, so try the move tentatively on your chosen rock first and then reassure your buddies that it is all OK. By doing this you can initiate a fun game of chicken and gain in confidence with the chosen rock.

Bear in mind what lies downstream of your rock, particularly since you are likely to exit from a splat upside down. No one really wants to run a huge waterfall capsized, no matter how cool the splat at the top looked! It is very handy to note that on higher volume rivers, hole type formations occur to the downstream of splattable rocks as water drops down the side of these rocks. These holes are usually accompanied by boily eddy lines and often share some of the nastier features of pourovers (difficult exits), so be sure to check out the downstream side as well as the upstream face of your chosen splat rock carefully.

Prerequisites

The only 'prereqs' to a splat are the ability to choose a safe spot and the ability to tail squirt. Practice on an eddy line near the rock before you go for it and you will be rehearsing the splat before you get close to the rock.

The Move

A splat is no more than a tail squirt which is performed upstream of a rock and presents the hull of your boat to the upstream face of the rock. Really good splat spots with strong cushion waves off the rock may sometimes stop you from actually touching the rock itself. Sky surfing on the cushion... Yes! If you get one of these you get numerous Brownie points and a big cheer from all your friends, as well as a good pub anecdote after the paddling session.

Timing the move is essential for a good splat, and although the actual dynamics are the same as for a tail squirt on an eddy line, it is a good idea to count through them since the consequences of messing up are much more severe.

As you approach your splat rock, try and keep your eyes focused on where you want to land your hull. Ideally, you should approach the rock slowly with the boat sideways onto the rock's cushion rather than paddling directly at the rock. You are trying to splat it rather than boof right over it!

As the boat drifts onto the cushion, begin the move. Reach downstream on a reverse sweep and edge the boat slightly upstream. The downstream blade will provide just enough support to prevent you from flipping.

Smoothly and fluidly, begin your sweep and maintain the upstream edge. The water pushing upstream from the cushion, combined with the tail squirt action of the upstream edge and reverse sweep, will push the stern of your boat underwater and lift the bow skywards.

Photo Sequence – Jim Shrimpton, Canolfan Tryweryn

Top - Note that the rock has a well defined cushion!
- The paddler approaches the rock almost side on. He is already looking at the splat spot and he controls the bow with a stern rudder on the downstream side.
- His upper body is turned toward the splat rock, building up pre-rotation.

Middle - As soon as the boat drifts onto the rock's cushion the stern rudder converts to a stern sweep.
- The boat is edged slightly upstream and the paddler's centre of gravity is loaded over the boat.
- The stern is pushed down on the cushion and the bow begins to rise to vertical.

Bottom - Splat! The bow is now vertical on the cushion.
- The stern sweep is then used to control the boat as it tracks toward the rock's exit area.

You can prolong the splat by supporting yourself on a vertical (sort of) support stroke, but the water will often drift you to the edge of the rock. This drift or tracking can be countered by edging the boat slightly in the opposite direction. This does, however, require considerable practice, and even then all bets are off.

As you exit off a splat all sorts of random things can happen; you may spin down the eddy line created by the rock (hurrah!), backloop, screw up, or simply land upright on the eddy line. Go out and experiment with H_2O!

Body

Throughout a splat it is a good idea to keep your eyes focused on (and your head turned toward) the area on the rock where you want your hull to hit it. Remember to keep your reverse sweep stroke fluid and maintain your upstream edge throughout the move. Do not overedge, as splats are unforgiving and you do not want to capsize onto your chosen rock. Do not tilt your body upstream during a splat as this will encourage a broach on the rock (see edging exercise). Finally, lean forward while splatting to counter a possible backloop on the rock's upstream face.

Boat

A good splat begins with the boat drifting sideways onto the rock's cushion wave, not powering toward the rock at full tilt. Slight upstream edge is usually enough to gain a good splat, since lifting the bow only slightly will force the stern underwater, even once the bow has contacted the rock. Slightly leaning the boat once you are splatting will counter any tracking and maintain a longer sky surf.

Blades

Don't be shy with your blades; reach far back in the reverse sweep and push smoothly to force the boat's stern underwater. It is possible to force a splat from a high brace if you edge the boat slightly more than usual and push down off an upstream high brace. This tends to be quicker than a splat initiated off a reverse sweep. The greater edge, cushion wave, and downstream drift will combine to capsize you if you hang about! From a stern sweep you have the advantage that, should you mistime the move, you can throw your weight onto the rock and use the downstream blade to brace onto the rock, saving you from a broaching scenario.

Common Mistakes

By far the most common error in this move is paddling full tilt at the rock. If you insist on doing this, it will reduce the replacement time of your boat by about a week every time you splat!

Other errors in this move seem to revolve around mistiming it. Be very careful with this and go back to eddy line tail squirts for a while to get your timing sorted, as edging upstream and failing to force the stern underwater may often lead to you broaching on the splat rock.

If you do find yourself drifting sideways on to the rock having mistimed a splat, act quickly. One good escape route is to flip dynamically upstream and roll onto the rock's upstream face. The low brace stern sweep is then already in position for a quick screw roll. This allows you to brace with your paddles on the rock and work your way to the escape route.

6.9 Rock Spins

Rock spins, like splats, are a fun but slightly dangerous move to include in your repertoire. Although it scores no points in competition, it can help turn even the most mundane flat water paddle into a full-on play battle with your friends.

A rock spin is the art of grounding your kayak on a midstream rock or sometimes on the river bank, spinning 360° or further whilst stalled, and then continuing downstream. 'Done right'.... the kayaker takes on the flair and aptitude of street skateboarders... 'done wrong' and... let's hope you brought that rescue kit!

Prerequisites

Choosing the right rock for a rock spin is difficult. The best rocks are few and far between, so let's start by looking at what to avoid.

1. Rocks which are sharp and can hole your precious kayak are well worth avoiding. One good spin isn't worth the expense of a new playboat.
2. Rocks which have close friends nearby. Say within a boat length on either side. You wouldn't want to broach across both rocks.
3. Rocks with too much moss on them. Moss, especially when dry, tends to stop you dead when you try and rock spin. Such a stall could cause you to slide down the upstream side of the rock and pin.

What you need is an isolated rock, slightly wet, smooth, and in the middle of the river away from any obstructions. Ideally your rock will poke about an inch or two out of the water but, if you are really lucky, it will sometimes be just covered by water (to aid your ride up onto it!).

Even when you have found your rock there is still no guarantee it is safe. I recently spun on a rock, cleared and put my blade deep to support, only to find that my paddle had snagged a rope which was strung around the rock itself... needless to say a brief struggle ensued. *Be careful!*

Boat skills

In order to pull off a good rock spin you need relatively few boat skills. We can all paddle forward and stick one blade in the water can't we? However, it is useful to at least have a working knowledge of stern squirts and have practised the bench spinning drill illustrated earlier in this book.

The Move

Let's start this move by assuming that you have selected your rock and are lined up ready to go for it. As you paddle toward the rock, the first thing to consider is the amount of speed you are going to use to hit the rock; too much and you'll bounce over it, too little and you could pin. In truth it is a good idea to use a little too much speed, since it is far more pleasant to ride over the rock than to be stuck on its upstream face. Keep your paddle strokes fluid and controlled, *do not* just go hell for leather. Remember, you want to look controlled.

The next thing you should consider is the angle at which you intend to attack the move. Assuming that you are going to spin with the current helping, you have two choices: you can either hit the rock straight on, or at a slight angle to the downstream current (about 20°). By hitting the rock at a slight angle, you can set up for the spin quite easily and maximise the amount of power you put into your final, but essential, stroke.

Let's assume you intend to strike at a slight angle. As you approach the rock, your final stroke should be on the upstream side of the boat. By pulling back reasonably hard on this final stroke, you can lift your bow so that it rides quite easily onto the rock. As soon as this stroke is finished, (often before the boat has fully grounded on the rock), reach back with the same blade so that it is ready for a reverse sweep stroke. Turn your shoulders so that they are parallel to the paddle shaft and start the boat spinning by planting this paddle into the downstream flow. As you do this, use the pressure on the blade to pull your legs around. You have initiated the spin and the hardest part is over!

Once the boat has started to spin, it is best to keep your weight as central as possible; you don't want the end of your boat to drop off the upstream side. You can continue spinning by forward sweeping on the opposite side from the initial stroke, much as you did during the bench spinning exercise.

Body

During the rock spin sequence you should keep your body weight as central over the boat as possible. Do not try to edge the boat during the spin but rather keep the hull of the boat flat on your pivot point.

As you begin the spin, your shoulders should be parallel to your paddle shaft. Once the blade is engaged in the downstream flow, use your stomach muscles to swing your legs around.

Boat

Keeping the hull of your boat as flat as possible on the rock is the key to extended rock spins. With a neutral edged boat and good pivot point it is possible to achieve an amazing number of rotations before you slide off the rock. A good spin will only come if both ends of the boat are lifted clear of the water so as to provide minimal resistance as the boat pivots around the rock.

Photo Sequence - Jim Shrimpton, Canolfan Tryweryn

Top - The angle of approach is about 20° across the downstream current.

- The paddler is approaching the rock quite fast; better to clear it altogether than to broach on it.

Bottom - Just before impact, the previous paddle stroke lifted the bow of the boat onto the rock.

- As the boat rides up onto the rock, the paddler 'winds up his body' and plants an assertive stroke at the upstream side stern of the boat. Timed right, this should cause the boat to spin as soon as both ends of the boat are clear of the water!
- Spintastic! The paddler continues the stern sweep throughout the move and *snaps* his head around to look over the upstream shoulder as the boat spins.

Blade

As you approach the rock, your final stroke will ideally be a strong forward stroke on the (slightly) upstream side of the boat. This will help the bow lift onto the rock and will set you up nicely to plant the next blade for the spin.

As soon as you begin to ride up the rock, before you stall, reach back with the same blade and plant it as far into the downstream flow as possible. *Do not* sweep this blade forward. Simply use it to provide pressure so that you can swing your legs around towards the blade.

Common Mistakes

By far the most common mistake in this move is bad rock selection. If you are in any doubt about your chosen rock, *leave it!* You can always come back when you are feeling more confident.

Another common mistake is failing to hit the rock with enough speed to either stall on the rock or clear it. This can result in a pin and is really the result of not being confident enough. By being under confident you are second guessing yourself and undermining the likelihood of you doing the move well; almost a self-fulfilling prophesy.

6.10 Pirouettes

This spectacular and difficult to master move has been neglected in recent years by the freestyle majority because it is seen as 'old school'. This is an undeserved neglect, since the move is not only difficult to master but scores high points in freestyle competition.

A pirouette is simply a vertical popout with a 360° or more spin on a vertical axis. To put it another way, once the boat has gone vertical, the boater causes the boat to spin on its nose much like a pirouetting ballet dancer. Exceptional boaters can cause the boat to spin twice or even three times around before landing upright.

Prerequisites

Before attempting to pirouette, a good controlled popout is essential. A good idea is to have practised the pre-rotation on a trampette or trampoline. Remember the exercise outlined earlier on in this book?

Try practising cross bow strokes to familiarise yourself with the correct paddle stroke sequence. One good exercise, to see how your paddle tends to drag your bow in the direction of the cross bow stroke, is to gently plant a cross bow rudder in the green water while you surf a small wave!

The Move

Start this move as you would a popout. Allow the boat to enter the green water slowly, keeping control using a stern rudder as you do so. This is very useful since, as the boat starts to rise to vertical, a strong sweep from the stern rudder will begin the boat spinning on its nose. In many holes this is usually sufficient to build up rotation and finish the entire pirouette. This is known as 'pre-rotation' since it is usually initiated *before* the boat reaches vertical and begins to spin.

As the boat reaches vertical you will be ideally leaning forward. Transfer the paddle from an aggressive (pushing down) stern rudder, to reach across your bow with the opposite blade, and plant it firmly in the downstream flow. Be careful at this point. Practice will tell you how much of your blade to plant, too much and you risk a dislocated shoulder. However, the more of this blade that is planted into the green water, the faster your pirouette will be and the more chance of multiple spins.

Timing at this point is critical. If you plant the blade too early and before you are vertical, you will probably flip dynamically and face-plant into the water. Too late and you will loop forward, with your paddle and shoulder in a vulnerable position. Try to get the blade in the water just as the boat is vertical; the bow will offer less resistance during the spin and you stand more chance of a double, or even the elusive triple pirouette.

As the boat begins to spin, stand upright on your footrest. This should prevent the boat from looping over and extend the amount of air time. Look sharply over your shoulder, swinging your shoulders in the same direction (the direction of travel), and pull the planted blade across your bow in a strong flowing motion... Spintastic!

Body

Initiate this move as you would a popout. Lean forward as you drop the bow into the green water and use the hips and knees to keep the boat flush to the downstream flow.

As the boat stands upright, concentrate on *standing* on your footrest and leaning back to control your landing and extend

Photo Sequence

- Jim Shrimpton, Tryweryn

This Page - The bow begins to purl down as in a popout and the boater increases pressure on the stern rudder creating pre-rotation.

Top Right - Once vertical the boater reaches across the bow and plants the paddle deep into the downstream flow. The kayak begins to spin!

Bottom Right - The boater stands on his footrest to control the boat from 'looping' over.
- Cross deck draw stroke is maintained.
- The paddler *looks* aggressively over the shoulder in the direction of the spin.

the air time. Snap your head to look over your shoulder in the direction in which you are travelling, and maintain this 'look' for the duration of the spin. Remember to swing your shoulders in the same direction to encourage the lower torso to follow the 'look'.

Boat

As the boat enters the green water it should be flush to the downstream flow. This will not only aid the bow's plunge, but help the volume in the boat push you upwards once the boat is 'standing'. Try and time the spin so that it takes place as the boat is as near vertical as possible. The bow will then offer only minimal resistance during the spin.

Blades

Enter the hole or wave with a stern rudder. This should keep the boat flush with the hole and can be easily transferred to a downward push stroke to initiate the boat's spin. This 'push' is often sufficient to spin the boat 360° on its nose without transferring to a cross bow stroke, especially when performing a pirouette in a hole rather than a pourover.

As the boat stands upright, change the stern rudder to a 'push' stroke and then plant the opposite blade across the bow into the downstream flow. Usually the downstream flow will be sufficient to spin the boat on its nose, but pulling the blade across the bow will speed up and maintain the spin to gain multiple pirouettes.

Common Mistakes

Timing is crucial to this move: too soon and you face plant as you spin, too late and you crash and burn with a loop. Try and time the move so that it takes place *only* when you are actually *standing* on your footrest.

Lack of commitment to the move can often lead to a disappointing pirouette. Don't be shy reaching across your bow. Failure to commit often leads to a 180° and clumsy looking single spin pirouette... Very ugly!

Coaching Points

Pirouettes change a simple popout into a scoring move or a really dramatic link move. Initially the popout has to be mastered as it's the base form of a pirouette.

The trick is to be able to adjust the speed in the spin. This allows you to use the move in a variety of ways. The closer you can get your body and paddles to the boat, the faster the spin. This is best achieved by standing on the footrest. To slow things down, extend your arms once you have the spin initiated.

Initiating the spin can be done in a variety of ways, but is primarily achieved with the paddle as either a cross deck or vertical paddle stroke.

The most common problem is that the boat is drawn off the vertical by the paddler over-reaching, i.e. moving the centre of gravity outside the boat. This is a difficult concept to visualise as the parameters of the boat are no longer defined by the gunwales. Picture someone standing on top of a telegraph pole. If they lean forwards, without bending their knees, what happens? They stick their bottom out to act as counter balance. If they didn't, what would happen? Try it. Stand with your back and heels against a wall and lean forwards from the hips. Now pick yourself up, stand a foot from the wall, and try the same thing. Is your bottom touching the wall?

7 Expert Moves

In a sense I am reluctant to define anything as 'for experts', since I tend to work on the theory that you are only as good as your next swim.

Expert (eks-pert) n. Ex - used to be - has been,
spert - small droplet of water placed under pressure.

Expert moves, as defined here, are all quite easy to master with enough practice, but can be 'wired' more easily if you take an analytical approach to your paddling sessions. When a move goes right, sit in the eddy for a while and ask yourself, "What did I do that was different from before?" By doing this you will soon start to understand the forces working on your boat to produce these moves. Another handy hint when progressing onto expert moves is to get a friend to video you in action and watch yourself carefully. Compare what you do to what the 'experts' do in your favourite boating video. Soon enough you may have a routine worth showing on video yourself.

Should you become seriously addicted to freestyle paddling, it may be a good idea to think of working closely with a coach. Although there are as yet no formal qualifications specifically aimed at freestyle coaching, there are a large number of highly qualified coaches who are more than capable of improving your freestyle technique. It's always handy to spend time having a highly trained pair of eyes spotting your moves and helping you improve. Many excellent coaches have contributed to this book and I unreservedly recommend them.

There is also a tendency for 'expert' paddlers to only become expert at their local playspot. It's understandable, due to ease of access, but if you really want to progress then it is a good idea to paddle at a variety of different spots on a regular basis and to spend as much time as possible searching out waves and holes which, to you, are new.

Performer's Top Tip

I started kayaking competitively from a very early age. I eventually realised that what I enjoyed about racing was the white water, and duly switched to running serious white water, both for a living and for personal kicks. But I approached white water in the same way as training for competitions.

In Austria I had two grade 4/5 sections that I used as my training ground. Every day I would run the sections at varying levels, making set moves down the rapids and playing in larger and larger holes. Then I would run other hard rivers when I felt good, running them several times, so I hadn't just survived the river but had paddled it and knew it intimately.

I looked at rock climbing and how hard serious climbers would train when they were attempting hard routes. If they weren't of the standard they wouldn't get off the ground. With kayaking anyone can put a boat in at the top and momentum will do the rest. Paddling with a clear and focused mind, making the moves the way I wanted and feeling at one with the water was my goal.

I also found it easy to become very good on my local sections, so I spent nine years out of the UK, finding the best white water worldwide (albeit in warm countries), so I could live by different rivers and meet up with like-minded paddlers. This stopped complacency, kept me working on new skill levels and was bloody good fun!

Colin Hill holds the Guinness Book of Records World Hand Rolling Record, paddles extreme white water worldwide and is recognised as a leading expedition kayaker and river runner. He is a member of the Eskimo / Playboater / Werner Pro Team.

7.1 One Armed Bandits

There are really two moves which people recognise as a bandit. They are defined as a one armed and a two armed bandit and, although very similar, are best described separately. Let's start with the one armed bandit.

This move usually takes place at the edge of a hole during a flat spin sequence. As the boat's bow begins to turn downstream, as in a flat spin, the boater kills the spin and pries the bow into the air so as to change the direction the boat faces from a downstream to an upstream one. It looks very spectacular and is used by advanced boaters to initiate moves such as cartwheels and splitwheels.

Prerequisites

It is a very good idea to have your flat spins well and truly sorted before advancing onto bandits. You should be quite familiar with the feeling of the spin and of when to transfer the edge of your boat to avoid the stern catching the green water. In a bandit the stern is allowed to 'catch', and the water pressure allowed to act upon it to help the bow rise and spin upstream.

It is also an excellent idea to be proficient at stern squirts on an eddy line before you begin banditing in a hole. Not only does this improve your edge control but it familiarises you with the feeling of an upstream edge 'catching', thus saving you from clumsy and unbalanced wipeouts.

The Move

In a one armed bandit the downstream blade, which is supporting you as you sit sideways in the hole, remains in the water throughout the move.

Start with a few flat spins and then go for it!

As the bow catches the downstream water rushing past the side of the hole, the bow will begin to turn downstream. Allow this turn to start as though you are simply flat spinning. By this time, you should be familiar with when to transfer your edge to avoid water piling up on your stern. The secret of a good bandit is to 'unlearn' this aspect of the flat spin and allow water to pile against your edged stern.

Once the bow has almost turned to face downstream, look over your (slightly) upstream shoulder (the shoulder which is *away* from the support blade) into the hole. This will give you a good view of your stern and help you to plant your bow exactly where you are looking, once the move has finished.

Just before you reach the point where you would normally transfer your edge (for a flat spin), bring your support blade close to the bow and push down on it quite aggressively. At the same time, increase your edge to reduce the resistance the hull presents to the hole's pile. This should have the effect of forcing the stern of the boat under the water (as it catches the green water) and, more importantly, under the 'pile' of the hole. At the same time initiate the boat's spin by looking more aggressively upstream.

Timed right, this sequence should raise the bow clear of the pile and kill the downstream spin, so that the direction in which the boat is spinning is reversed. As the boat spins round to face upstream the bow will be elevated, creating a spectacular arc.

You should ideally finish this move facing upstream with the support blade now acting as a stern rudder. Many freestyle paddlers use a one armed bandit to initiate a cartwheel sequence; indeed I have heard some women paddlers argue that, with their lower centre of gravity, it is easier for a woman to initiate cartwheels like this than by planting the bow down.

Body

As in a flat spin, the one armed bandit starts by side surfing the hole. Your body should be relaxed with the upstream knee raised to avoid the upstream edge catching. Lean forward to initiate the bow turning downstream, and look over your upstream shoulder so as to watch the stern of the boat, just as you would during a flat spin.

Remember that it is handy to think about edging as though you are balancing on your downstream buttock as much as raising the upstream knee. Such ideas help you maintain your balance while side surfing and can lead to faster progression to bandits.

Slightly before the boat reaches the point where, in a flat spin, you would transfer edges, reach forward and look into the hole with an aggressive head snap. If you edge the boat at this point, the degree the bow is raised should be quite significant and more aesthetically pleasing. Remember to keep looking at where you are going to plant the bow throughout the move.

Photo Sequence - John 'Pies' Smith, Hurley Weir

Top - Start with a nice relaxed side surf in the hole.
Middle - The bow of the boat begins to turn downstream.
- Reach forward on the original support blade and plant as for a high brace.
- Begin to drop the boat on edge by edging *toward* the hole's pile and *look* over the shoulder away from the high brace stroke.
Bottom - Push down assertively on the high brace and drive the edged stern under the hole's pile.
- The bow arcs back upstream to land facing the hole's ramp. (Time to cartwheel?)

Boat

As in a flat spin, the boat should be edged with the upstream edge out of the green water. When the boat begins to spin, increase this edge so that the stern provides less resistance when it is forced underwater.

Practice will tell you when the optimum time is to begin the move. It is usually just before (by milliseconds) the usual time of edge transference. Performed correctly, a one armed bandit will force the bow clear of the water and the stern under the hole's pile, thus helping you retain the wave. The more you edge the boat, the less resistance the stern will provide to the green water flowing under the hole, making the move more spectacular as the bow arcs round and preventing the boat from washing out of the hole.

Blades

Side surfing in a hole requires a steady and relaxed low brace. Forward and reverse strokes will help initiate the spin.

Just as the stern begins to catch, change your low brace to a high brace close to the bow as you increase the downstream edge. This high brace will provide enough support to finish the move.

As the stern catches, pull back on this high brace support. This paddle action will lift the bow out of the water and should continue as the bow arcs through the air, so that you land with the same blade acting as a stern rudder.

Common Mistakes

Edging the boat too late will dynamically flip the boat upstream with your paddles in a vulnerable high brace position... Ouch!

Edging too early will prevent the bow from carving fluidly through the air, and you will wind up side surfing the hole in your original position. Insufficient pressure throughout the move on your support blade will have much the same effect. These small errors in your paddling will often go hand in hand, so try counting in your head so that you get the timing wired.

Failing to edge the boat sufficiently will cause a greater surface area of the stern to be presented to the green water. This will usually result in a back loop and a disappointing but spectacular exit from the playhole.

7.2 Two Armed Bandits

Although very similar in appearance and technical difficulty to its one armed cousin, the two armed bandit is a move in its own right. Thorough practice of the two armed bandit will help you start to learn the holy grail of the freestyle kayaker... the cartwheel. This is because the moves involved are almost the same as the second end in a bow-first two point cartwheel, or the first move in a stern-first cartwheel. Many freestyle kayakers begin cartwheeling stern first, initiating the whole sequence with a two armed bandit.

Prerequisites

Like the one armed bandit it is a very good idea to be proficient at stern squirts before venturing onto this move. These will teach you how much upstream edge you can handle before capsizing upstream, an essential element in a two armed bandit, as you will edge upstream at the side of a hole to start the move.

Since this move is often started from a flat spin in a hole, you should be good at this before you attempt a two armed bandit.

The Move

As you begin your flat spin, the bow will catch the green water at the edge of the hole and start to spin downstream. Keep your eyes on the hole by looking over your upstream shoulder.

Just before you would transfer edges for a flat spin, drop your upstream edge slightly and change support blades from a downstream low brace support to a dynamic (slightly) upstream high brace and pull back sharply on this blade. If you have timed the move correctly, the green water should catch your stern and lift the bow clear of the pile; too soon and you will flip upstream having caught too much green water. When done correctly, dropping the upstream edge of your boat in this manner will allow the stern to slice under the hole's pile, the green water rushing under the hole having caught the upstream edge of the stern.

If you pull back on the now upstream high brace, the pressure on the blade combined with the water piling onto the stern should pull the boat vertical on the stern. The deck of the boat will, in this move, face the end of the hole and usually the river bank.

As the boat goes vertical, take the pressure off the high brace support and look over the opposite shoulder with a head snap. Quickly change blades onto the opposite paddle and pull forward with a forward paddle stroke. This will help you stay in the hole and allow you to land upright and facing upstream, with your blades acting as a stern rudder. Watch a video of expert boaters pulling cartwheels and you will often see them using this forward pull stroke to retain the hole and initiate even more ends.

At first it will seem strange to go through this sequence of looking into the hole, head snap and changing pressure on your blades. Practice and timing will make the move seem more instinctive and natural.

Body

A handy tip when learning to two armed bandit is to look into the hole over your upstream shoulder as long as possible. Only snap your head around and look over the opposite shoulder once you can see the hole no more, typically once the boat has got past vertical and the bow is beginning to drop back down into the hole.

Edging upstream before you would for a flat spin may go against your instincts at first but, with a little practice, you will know how much water you can allow onto your stern without flipping you upstream. Remember to reach forward assertively as soon as you drop your edge upstream, and to lean forward throughout the move. This allows the boat to rotate smoothly around your body, protecting you should you flip in the hole.

Photo Sequence - Steve Whetman - Photos: Helen Metcalfe / Nookie
Top - Ease the bow into the green water as for a flat spin.
Top Right - Reach forward on the original support blade and plant as for a high brace.
  - Drop the boat on edge by edging *away* from the hole's pile and *look* over the shoulder away from the high brace stroke.
Middle - Pull back on the high brace and maintain the upstream edge to bring the boat vertical.
Bottom - Look over opposite shoulder, change blades and pull the boat back into the hole with a forward power stroke.

Boat

Edging the boat at the critical time is essential in this move. There should be just enough water piling onto the stern to lift the bow, and enough edge to allow the paddle to help the bow arc through the air to an upstream facing direction.

In very modern playboats less than a few inches of water need to pile onto the stern for this move. The combination of very low volume ends and sharp rails allow the stern to slice underwater with very little green water assisting. Try going for a bandit sequence in an eddy or on the flat to see just how little water the stern need ship. Paddle backwards in a relaxed manner, and then edge the boat while at the same time reaching forward to plant the paddle close to the bow, with the drive face of the paddle pushing down. By doing this you should easily force the stern underwater and the bow should arc upward and around... *Flat water spins!*

Blades

While side surfing keep your blades in a low brace position. As soon as you allow the upstream edge to drop, transfer this low brace to an upstream high brace support. (Against your instincts isn't it!). This should provide enough support to prevent you flipping. As your bow at this point is facing almost downstream, the upstream brace should actually be planted on the hole's pile, rather than on the ramp as the term 'upstream brace', might imply.

Immediately pull back on this high brace support as the bow starts to rise, and maintain the pressure on this blade as the boat rises so that the bow goes vertical.

As the bow reaches vertical the 'two armed' aspect of this move comes into play. Take the pressure off the high brace support and change blades so that, as the bow drops, you pull forward with a kind of vertical forward stroke. This should help you retain the hole and, once you have followed this stroke through, acts as a low brace support stroke upon landing.

Common Mistakes

Presenting too much of your stern, caused by dropping your upstream edge too soon, will have two possible effects:

1. You may flip upstream and have to quickly power roll to stay in the hole.
2. The bow will go vertical but your body will be hanging slightly under the boat, again causing you to land upside down and forcing a power roll, a sort of elevated flip.

Failing to change blades as the boat goes vertical, or leaving it too late will probably allow you to blow out of the hole, or may leave you on the brink of the hole's pile, forcing you to quickly forward paddle upon landing to reattain the hole.

7.3 Retendos

I first saw this move described as a 'Polish Pirouette' in a late eighties text showing survival techniques for river running. Indeed it is a handy way to stay upright when getting worked in a hole. However, when done in a controlled way, it is a useful ally in a freestyle repertoire, since it usually prevents the boater from washing out of the hole and wasting vital competition seconds paddling up the eddy.

The move starts by looking very like a loop or popout. Then, as the stern rises, the boater's body torque twists the boat and reduces the amount of catch on the bow, allowing him or her to remain in the hole and typically resulting in a side surf.

Prerequisites

A good controlled loop will help you master this move. Combine this with the ability to edge your boat, side surf, and roll fast, and you should have this move sorted quite quickly.

The Move

Essentially a retendo is little more than an elevated power flip, allowing the bow to catch the green water and the stern to arc through the air while the roll is executed.

Initially this move is exactly the same as a front loop. Allow the bow to catch and continue leaning forward as the stern rises. It may help if the boat is slightly edged upstream as the bow plunges, but you can transfer to a downstream edge once the bow has entered the green water. By edging the boat during the move, you allow the bow to plunge quickly but, as you twist the boat so that it is edged, you will shed this green water off your deck and the bow will slice through the hole's pile. This reduces your chances of a 'popout' or worse.... blowing out of the hole altogether.

As you edge the boat downstream, keep pressure on your downstream paddle and twist your body downstream so that you throw the boat's stern around your body. When the boat begins to twist, change blades so that they arc around your body. The action of transferring blades from this brace on the hole's pile on one side to the other is very much like punching down onto the hole's pile with the fist which was held across your body. This motion should spin the boat so that it lands flat side surfing the hole and the now downstream blade acts as a low brace support upon landing.

It is important to remember during this move that the whole thing relies upon your body torque to twist the boat from a vertical to a horizontal axis. One freestyle paddler describes the move as though you are throwing the boat over your shoulder like a sack of potatoes. *Note: When a cartwheel looks as though the boater is over rotating on the front end, it is possible to stop the back end from entering the green water and washing you out of the hole by changing the cartwheel to a retendo; all it needs is a little more rotation to land you sideways in the trough.*

Body

During a retendo the boat rotates around the kayaker's body. You should concentrate on leaning forward to initiate the loop, remaining focused on the hole (to encourage your boat to land there). Remember the golden rule of *looking* at the point where you intend to land the boat. Transfer your forward lean to a lean on the pile once vertical. To achieve the final complex lean, edge your boat downstream by lifting your upstream knee once you are beginning to go vertical, and twist your upstream blade around and under your body so that you are bracing on the pile.

During the body sequence of a retendo, it is a good idea to think of the body talk as though you are keeping your shoulders parallel to your paddle shaft. Therefore as you transfer your paddle braces, you are twisting your body in tune with them.

Photo Sequence - Bill Mattos, Canolfan Tryweryn
Above - Setting up the bow to dive.
Top Right - Swinging the boat in a vertical arc.
Middle Right - Landing and bracing on the pile.
Bottom Right - Finishing in a side surf.

Boat

Controlling your boat in the vertical plane is essential to a smooth retendo; try and flick the boat's stern around your body once the bow is submerged, since it then provides less resistance to the green water. Remember that the stern of the boat should arc through the air about 270°, swinging up and around to come from an upstream surfing position to a side surfing position. As you land you will feel the edge of the stern begin to catch. It is then time to edge the boat so that you side surf rather than try and force the second end of a cartwheel. To try and push the stern underwater at this point will allow the stern to catch excessively and probably flip you.

Blades

Much of the rotation during a retendo comes from your blades. In fact the body rotation is led by the blades, so try and keep your shoulder line parallel with your paddle shaft.

Start with a slight brace on your downstream blade as you allow the bow to plunge. This will load the boat with pre-rotation and facilitate an easier transfer onto your edge as you go vertical. As the bow plunges into the green water and the stern begins to rise, swing the upstream blade, (the one which you had *not* been bracing on), across your chest, almost as though you are going for a cross bow draw stroke as in a pirouette. Instead of dabbing the blade into the green water as you would in a pirouette, allow the cross bow to follow through and brace on the hole's pile, almost throwing the boat over your upstream (slightly) shoulder and into a side surf once it lands.

Common Mistakes

By far the most common mistake during a retendo is the temptation to 'go for it', try to cartwheel and allow the stern to catch the green water as it lands. Many boaters do this in the mistaken belief that, by allowing the stern to catch, the boat will give them a two point cartwheel before they wash out. Remember, the retendo is a very forceful move compared to a cartwheel, and is more similar in nature to a splitwheel. It requires greater rotation on the bow, so trying to force a cartwheel when you initially went for a retendo will probably land your stern clear of the optimum spot for the stern to plant. This forces too much green water onto the stern and blows you out of the hole (usually upside down). Retendos are a good building block for progression onto cartwheels so practice these first; they develop your spatial awareness, and get you used to the weirdness of flying in a kayak and landing upright in a hole.

7.4 Blasts

This move, like many others in the modern float boat repertoire, evolved out of squirt boating. While high volume float boats were limited to surfing green waves, low volume squirt boats could rip it up, even on broken waves or holes, by surfing the ramp forming the hole, with the stern of their boats under the hole itself. It wasn't long, however, before float boats with increased paddler ability and decreased volume began blasting.

Prerequisites

As far as boat design is concerned, nearly all freestyle specific designs from the last five years have the ability to pull off a blast, especially those with a reasonably low volume stern.

Boaters, however, have a larger number of 'prereqs' to deal with before attempting a blast. The ability to control the boat well during a front surf and to use body leans to control position on a wave is essential. Since you will often end a blast by side surfing a hole, the ability to hole ride and more importantly the ability to escape your chosen hole, is also a necessity.

The Move

It is possible to start blasting in two ways: the pry, and what we will refer to here as the 'shunt'.

The Pry

To begin a blast with a pry, you will usually begin side surfing in a hole. Try to choose a hole without a steep ramp, where you feel comfortable side surfing with very little pressure on your downstream (support) blade.

Once comfortable and ready to go for it, release the support blade so that you are side surfing without a blade in support. With the upstream blade reach up and back, placing the reverse face of the blade as far back toward your upstream stern as you can without hyper-extending your arm. This last point is especially worth emphasising, since any upstream flip while reaching back in this way is liable to pull that precious shoulder straight out of its socket, and then you'll be stuck in the hole with a dysfunctional arm!

If you reach back and turn your body trunk at the same time, you will be 'wound up' ready to engage the blade and force the pry. By inserting this upstream blade into the green water forming the ramp, the stern of your boat, currently sideways on in the hole, will be forced underwater. You will then end up surfing upstream with the boat's bow skipping on top of the ramp. Congratulations, you are now blasting!

The Shunt

The second way of forcing the boat into a blast requires a much less complex sequence than the 'pry'. Simply hold the boat on the hole's pile and then, when you want to blast, lean forward using your paddle as a stern rudder to keep you straight. The next element, if you are to avoid a popout, is timing. As the boat drops down the pile, use your stomach muscles to lift the bow so that it clears the maw and rides up the ramp into a perfect blast position. Transferring the stern rudder into an assertive forward stroke as you drop into the blast, will help lift the bow clear of the ramp.

Holding the Blast

Having succeeded in getting your boat into a blasting position all you have to do now is hold it there. The first thing to remember is to lean forward. In very low volume boats, failing to lean forward far enough can lead to a back loop, whereas leaning too far forward can push the bow into the ramp, a sure recipe for a good 'trashing'.

Next matter to consider is preventing the boat from either tracking or falling prematurely back into a side surf. To do this use the blade that pried you into position as a vertical stern rudder. Compensate for any track by pulling the rudder close to the boat, or conversely, pushing the blade out and away from the boat. Don't worry if this sounds a little compli-cated, it comes more naturally than you think.

Body

While side surfing in the hole, the upstream knee should be raised to prevent any edges from catching. This edge should be maintained until the boat faces upstream in order to prevent a dynamic flip halfway through the sequence. As you reach around to begin the pry, try and turn as much of your body to face upstream as possible and look at where you intend to land your bow. You will consequently be 'wound up' for the move and have built up that all important pre-rotation. Try and keep your shoulder line parallel to your paddle shaft throughout this sequence so that, as you reach around with your blade, your body twists and builds up pre-rotation.

As you pry the boat into a blast, lean forward. The whole of the underside of the boat is skimming on the hole's ramp at this point. While it is surprisingly easy to back loop off a blast in a steep hole, the surface area of the hull of the boat makes catching the front end of the boat in the green water very unlikely. Conversely, in a hole which has a less sharply

See: 7.5 Blasting Transitions for photo sequence.

inclined ramp your greatest danger is catching the bow, so lean back a little and use your stomach muscles to lift the bow out of the green water.

Boat

The side surf edge of the boat should be maintained until the bow points upstream. This is because this edge allows the stern of the boat to naturally slice under the hole's pile with very little resistance.

Blades

While side surfing the hole, you will usually be supporting on your downstream blade. Try and reduce the amount of pressure you put on this blade, so that eventually you can comfortably side surf with hardly any, or ideally, no pressure on this blade.

Prying the stern down means that you have to reach back toward the upstream stern and insert the now upstream blade into the green water rushing down the hole's ramp. Be careful here. If you insert too little of this blade you will be unstable on your downstream edge and probably over tilt downstream. Conversely, if you insert too much blade, excessive amounts of green water will pile onto the blade and pull you over upstream in a very vulnerable position.

Once you have pushed the stern underwater, use the pry blade as a vertical stern rudder to control drift in the hole. By doing this, you can sustain a blast for an incredible amount of time, annoying all those waiting in the eddy queue.

Common Mistakes

By far the most common mistake when trying to pry the bow into a blast is attempting the move too ambitiously. In a steep ramped hole you are likely to lose downstream support, tip slightly downstream and then overcompensate using your knees so that an upstream edge catches and… Ouch!

Similarly, inserting too much blade face into the upstream ramp while prying will likely drag you over upstream with a similar effect.

To avoid either of these, try the move in a hole with a gentler ramp and where the water pressure is fairly gentle. Get used to the move before you get ambitious. Remember, always have your arms slightly bent, so that when the inevitable happens and you do flip upstream, your arms stay where they are supposed to be… attached to your shoulders!

When initiating the blast from a 'shunt', the most common mistake is mistiming and, by allowing the bow to purl in the maw of the hole, causing a popout. Practice lifting the bow here with a slight forward lean, but don't think of it as a forward lean, rather as lifting the bow using your stomach muscles.

7.5 Blasting Transitions

A blasting transition is actually quite a simple move which looks very spectacular when performed in control. Quite simply, it is a cartwheel performed across the ramp so that the boat's deck is parallel with the hole formed by the ramp.

Prerequisites

Let us assume that you already know how to blast; you aren't going to get very far with blasting transitions if you don't!

Happy with blasting? Now go and ensure that your eddy line cartwheels are reasonably up to scratch. The sequence of moves used in this trick are very similar to those of a cartwheel so you may as well practice them too!

The Move

Let's assume that you have succeeded in getting the blast wired and can hold it comfortably in your chosen hole. You should be leaning forward and have your blade held in a vertical stern rudder.

Allow the boat to fall sideways into the hole by simply reducing the pressure on your blade, and allowing the boat to fall to the side on which you were ruddering. As the bow begins to arc downward, look down into the hole, encouraging the bow to land at the spot where you are looking.

Don't be tempted to transfer the vertical stern rudder into a conventional downstream low brace. Instead, as soon as the boat lands side on in the hole, push down with the downstream blade and lean forward hard. This blade should be close to the boat and quite near your hips in order to be most effective. Throughout this, remember to keep the boat on edge, just as you would if you ended the front blast with a side surf.

The edge, forward lean, and paddle push will force the bow of the boat under the hole's pile so that you have changed from a back blast to a front blast, e.g. from blasting with the stern submerged to blasting with the bow submerged.

Performer's Top Tip

From a sustained blast you have to throw the boat round as hard as you can, so that the releasing hull spins around to stay on the green area in front of the hole.

Martin Tapley paddles for Wavesport, Nookie and Reed Chillcheater.

While the bow is submerged keep leaning forward; it is easy at this point to catch a stern edge. If your blades are feathered favourably (45° or even less), you can support this front blast by pushing downward on both blades.

To continue cartwheeling across the hole, allow the boat's stern to fall back toward the side surf position; simply hip flick the boat in your chosen direction and it'll drop. As soon as you are side surfing, pull sharply down on a high brace stroke on the downstream side of the boat. This stroke is most effective beginning close to your knees. The effect will be much the same as throwing the boat into a back blast from a high brace, almost as though you had high braced the boat into a blast in the first place.

Body

Throughout a blasting transition the body should be leaning forward. This will prevent a back loop in the initial phase of the move in a steep hole, and keep the bow from purling while in the second phase of the move, thus preventing your stern from catching the green water.

Consecutive drops back into the hole (sideways on) are controlled using hip flicks toward the direction in which you want to drop.

As the boat drops from a back blast, a sharp forward lean will encourage the bow to sink down, right in the hole's 'squeeze'. Lean forward as the boat drops into a front blast.

Photo Sequence (overleaf)- Bleddyn Lloyd, Canolfan Tryweryn

Top Left - Boat in a forward blast, note the hull is presented evenly to the hole's ramp and is kicking up to vertical.
- Stern rudder keeps the blast stable and prevents the boat falling into a side surf until desired.

Middle Left - Boat begins to fall into a side surf.
- Paddler reaches back to stern with blades on side of fall, and winds up body to push stern into a blast.
- Note that the paddler is looking at where the bow is soon to fall.

Bottom Left - Paddler loads weight onto the bow to aid it sinking.
- Boat held on edge throughout to allow it to slice down in the 'squeeze'.
- Downstream blade held behind the body and pushes *down* on a low brace stroke to force the bow down (just like in the second part of the 'double pump').

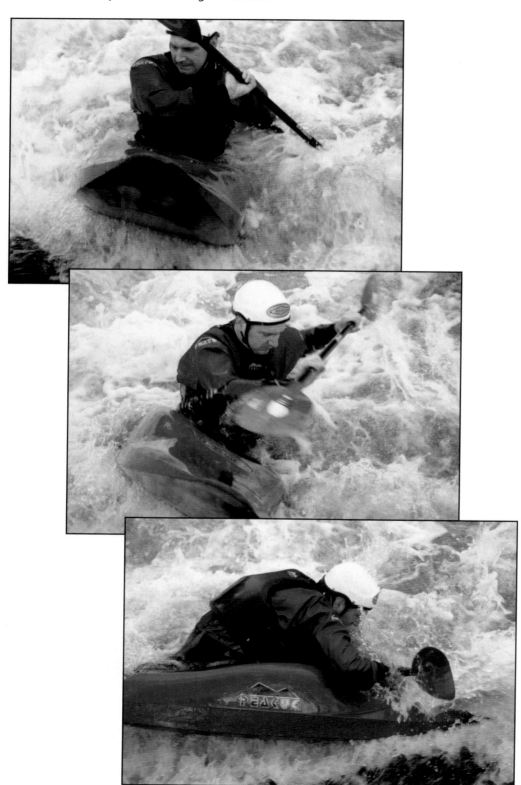

Boat

While actually blasting, the boat should be held flush to the hole's ramp with little or no edge. Edging the boat in this position would encourage the boat to track across the hole.

While getting into either front or back blast positions, try and hold the boat on edge, as this will allow the boat's ends to slice cleanly under the hole's pile and into blast positions nicely.

Blades

The blade action involved in a blasting transition is almost identical to that of a flat water cartwheel. As the bow drops back down to a side surf position, reach around with the whole upper body, and push down on a low brace close to your hips. This will encourage the bow to sink under the pile and lift the stern into a back blast. As your body talk causes the stern to drop, a high brace pull close to your knees will push the stern under the pile and you will end up front blasting again! Repeat as appropriate.

Common Mistakes

Catching your edges during any part of this sequence will result in a dynamic flip. You are especially vulnerable as the bow or stern drops back into a side surf, so practice lifting your upstream knee slightly as you drop.

Photo Sequence (overleaf) - Continued

Top Right - Body weight still loaded onto bow as boat transitions into a back blast.
- Both paddles push down on the water and provide stability on *both* sides (only possible when using blades with very little 'feather' e.g. 45° or less).

Middle Right - Stern begins to fall back into side surf.
- Paddler lands on a high brace *close* to the edged boat and pushes down on this stroke to force the stern down into the 'squeeze'.
- Body weight has shifted back to lift the bow clear of the hole's ramp.

Bottom Right - Back into a front blast! Note how the paddler immediately inserts a stern rudder and stabilizes the front blast.

7.6 Eddy Line Cartwheels

In modern (fifth generation and later) playboats, it is as easy to cartwheel on an eddy line as it is in a hole. Indeed, one of the best places to practice the sequence of complicated movements needed for a cartwheel in a hole is on the eddy lines; less chance of getting 'trashed', less water piling onto your deck, and thus more time to get the stroke sequence wired.

An eddy line cartwheel is the art of pulling an ender on entering or leaving an eddy, holding this ender on edge and then allowing the boat to arc around from a front ender to a back ender and back to a front ender. This sequence can be repeated until it becomes tedious.

Prerequisites

Before trying this move ensure that you are comfortable playing on eddy lines and can roll with ease on your chosen eddy fence. Remember that eddy lines are often areas of 'funny' water, and that rolling may sometimes be problematic. Make sure that your edge control is up to scratch, and that you can smash both bow and stern into the water as in the oscillating exercise at the start of this book.

The oscillating exercise (double pump) is the basis of good cartwheels, so make sure that your double pump is fine tuned.

Get used to your chosen eddy line by practising a few tail squirts, cut backs or other such variations, before going for the eddy line cartwheel.

The Move

This move can be done either entering the eddy, or on exit. Let's assume it's being done on entry.

Paddle at the eddy with a little forward speed, keeping your hull flat on the water. In many modern boats even paddling at speed will cause water to pile onto the deck, but you really don't want to start this move by 'shovelling' in this manner. An eddy line cartwheel is reliant on edge control for grace.

Performer's Top Tip

I guess the best thing about a cartwheel is it's such a fluid move. A good top tip is to go hard at it, it's an aggressive move; commit fully to it!

Jonny Pearson won the British Men's Freestyle Champs. in 1997, has paddled many extreme rivers around the world and has a list of sponsors such as Pyranha, Palm, Rough Stuff, Mean Scream and Five Ten.

The Approach

As the boat enters the eddy it should really be at a very shallow angle to the eddy line, almost, but not quite, as though you are going to skirt the eddy without actually entering it.

About half a boat length from the eddy line, tilt the boat on edge (the edge nearest the eddy), keeping your centre of gravity over the boat and not hanging out to the side. If you have got quite a bit of speed up, your body will usually be able to hang further out from the boat's centre of gravity than it would were you edging while side surfing a hole. This is best compared to leaning into the turn while you ride a bicycle; with practice your body can lean quite far away from the boat without reducing the balance.

The Lift

Lift the bow by pulling back on a strong high brace stroke. Not only will this give you plenty of support while on edge but, combined with the release of water provided by edging the boat, the high brace stroke should lift the bow clear of the water, since it pushes down rather than around and away from the boat. While on edge, keep your paddle blade as close as possible to the edged side of the boat to maximise the bow's lift and pull back on the paddle as far as possible. Again your shoulders should be parallel to your blade shaft, so that the strength of your 'abs' (abdominal muscles) is brought into play through the paddle talk.

The Smash

As soon as you have pulled back so that the blade is just behind your hips, there will be a brief moment of instability and the slightly raised bow will begin to fall. At this essential moment, change the high brace 'pull' stroke to a low brace 'push' stroke, again close to the boat. Remember to push down into the water with each stroke and don't allow the blade to travel away from the boat. This will provide some much needed support and will increase the rate at which the bow falls. In squirt boating terminology this is known as a 'smash', and timed right should have the effect of slamming the bow's edge down into the water.

Throughout the 'smash', lean your body forward and endeavour to stand on your foot-rest. With a good smash and excellent timing you should be able to get vertical on the front end, right on the eddy line. It is very good style at this point to *look* at the point where you are smashing the bow down into the water, encouraging the boat to follow this 'look'.

The Slam

Keep leaning forward during this phase of the eddy line cartwheel to keep your centre of gravity low and increase your support. As soon as your boat reaches its optimum height, reach down to the water with the opposite blade from the one which initiated the smash, and pull sharply back across your bow. This high brace stroke will pull the bow out of the water and should slam the stern down into the eddy line. The stern releases quite easily since it is edged throughout the move, and is thus able to shed water easily.

The transition from smashing the bow into the water to slamming the stern down usually happens very quickly and is best done at an angle of about 60° or 70° rather than 90°. This not only looks more controlled, but sets you up for a dry landing or even, if you're good, continued cartwheels.

Getting the Third End

Getting the third end on an eddy line cartwheel begins when the stern is slammed into the water for the second end. The bow at this point should be pointing toward the sky and you should be high bracing on the paddle which threw the stern down.

More Ends

To continue cartwheeling, as soon as the bow reaches to its optimum height, transfer your paddle power from the high brace and across your body onto a low brace on the opposite side of your boat. This will have the effect of bringing the bow down from vertical as soon as possible. Low brace with an assertive push downward and look at where you want to plant the bow of your boat. This low brace should help maintain the boat's edge, and speed the bow's rate of descent, setting you up for another 'smash' and continued ends. Remember to keep your shoulders parallel to your paddle shaft and reach as far as you can around your body. By doing this, your momentum and pre-rotation will be preserved so that the continued ends are fluid and smooth. The sooner you reach around and onto a low brace, the faster your bow will drop and the more effective this next 'smash' will be.

Body

To initiate this move keep the boat's hull on an even keel, paddling forward until about half a boat length from your chosen eddy line.

At this distance, bring the boat on edge using your hips and knees while endeavouring to keep your body weight over the boat's centre of gravity. The faster you are travelling, the more your body can hang out over the side of the boat without upsetting your balance.

Lean back slightly while your paddle pulls the bow up to initiate the 'smash', and then, still on edge, lean hard forward to stand on your footrest as the bow plunges. *Look* at the point where you have driven the bow down and lean forward throughout.

As the stern begins to drop, *look* again over your shoulder toward the falling stern. As your stern drops, your body will twist away from the eddy. At this point, *snap* your head to look over the opposite shoulder. If you do this quickly you should actually see the stern drop down under the water.

Boat

As you paddle toward the eddy line, the boat should be flat on the water with a little water piling onto the front deck. Enter the eddy at a very shallow angle, almost as though you were going to skirt the eddy without entering it. The shallower the angle of entry, the less water spinning upstream in the eddy will pile on your deck, and the eventual move should be slower and more controlled.

Photo Sequence - Bill Mattos - Photos: Helen Metcalfe / Nookie

The following sequence is of a flat water cartwheel. The sequence is the same as for an eddy line cartwheel except that without the help of a eddy line, greater precision and effort is required.

Top Left - Approaching the eddy line or on flat water simply getting up speed.

Middle Left - Edging the boat and lifting the bow on a high brace.

Bottom Left - Maintaining edge and driving the bow underwater. Note his head is well forward.

Top Right - As the boat comes upright the body comes more upright ready for the transition.

Middle Right - Reaching across the bow to pull the stern down.

Bottom Right - Vertical on the stern and about to reach around to initiate the third end.

About half a boat length from your eddy, tilt the boat on edge and lift the bow with an assertive front sweep stroke. The bow should rise considerably out of the water and then drop sharply, still on edge, 'smashing' the bow into the water.

Once the bow has plunged and the stern has arced around, it will begin to drop away and smash into the water smoothly. Keeping the boat on edge throughout this sequence will make the move smoother and enable continued ends in a very smooth style.

Blade

Throughout this move the blade serves three purposes: speed, control, and support.

Lift the bow with a strong sweep stroke close to the boat and deep into the water. As soon as this forward sweep loses power, switch from the blade's power face and push downward on the reverse face using a low brace, as you would during a 'double pump'. This low brace push stroke should support you on edge and throw the edged bow deep into the water.

Continue pushing on this low brace stroke until you once again lose power and the stern arcs out of the water to begin dropping. Then reach across your bow with the opposite blade and draw it sharply across your bow. This will pull the stern down and once again 'smash' your edged boat (the stern this time) into the eddy line.

Continue cartwheeling by maintaining the boat's edge and, using the power of gravity to help 'smash' the bow into the eddy line, by pushing sharply down on another low brace as soon as the bow begins to drop. Remember, the sooner you reach around once the bow is airborne, the more power your low brace paddle will build, and the faster your third end will be.

Common Mistakes

Shovelling

This is a clumsy looking, yet quite effective technique used by those whose edge control is not up to scratch. In very modern playboats, simply paddling hard whilst leaning forward will cause considerable amounts of water to pile onto the deck and lift the stern out of the water; not so much a 'mistake', rather a clumsy way of initiating an eddy line cartwheel.

Over-edging

Over-edging, especially edging the boat to an angle beyond 90° to the horizontal has two effects:

1. a dramatic capsize or, if you manage to smash the bow down,
2. a dramatic eddy line front loop.

Although there is merit in the latter of these, it is not nearly as fluid as a smooth eddy line cartwheel. The solution to this problem is simply to *relax*. A good eddy line cartwheel with the boat cartwheeling at 60° or 70° looks far more controlled than a vertical flop in and flail.

Capsizing upon Initiation

This is common amongst those who are not confident on edge, or feel uneasy about allowing their paddle to support them on edge. Go back to the oscillating exercise and practice until the point of boredom (in some cases this may last for years). When you are confident on edge, go back to the eddy line and try again.

7.7 Cartwheels and Variations

This was the move of the nineties, a move which revolutionised freestyle boating as we knew it at the 1993 Ocoee World Championships, and became the focus of freestyle for the rest of the decade. This resulted in a host of new variations, ranging from cartwheeling down the back of a wave (wavewheel), to cartwheeling off the lip of a waterfall (hammer, freewheel). The sport had changed completely, and boating manufacturers responded by changing the emphasis of their designs. Nowadays boats are designed to slice through the water cleanly, enabling such variations as flat water and eddy line cartwheels.

Prerequisites

Since cartwheeling is a hybrid of many moves, it is very useful to have a proficient freestyle repertoire before moving onto it. One of the main stumbling blocks of aspirant cartwheelers is that they place too much emphasis on this move, and tend to neglect the rest. This has resulted in compulsory variety moves at most competitions in order to prevent the sport becoming mere 'cartwheel contests', a criticism levelled at the Augsburg 1995 World Championships.

In order to move onto cartwheels, make sure that you are comfortable side surfing holes on both sides, that your bandit moves are up to scratch, that you are happy in the vertical plane and, ideally, comfortable with the concept of retendos. In short you should be a good all round boater willing to give it a try.

The Move

This move is traditionally done in a hole, although radical boat design and advanced boat skills have recently made a cartwheel attainable on almost any river feature.

In a hole, the move can be started from either end, although I prefer a bow initiation. A stern initiation tends to start with a two armed bandit, arcing the bow across to land facing upstream and ready to 'smash' down for another end.

For a bow initiation, sit high on the hole's pile with the boat angled slightly across the hole, as if you are going to ferryglide across the pile. In this position one side of the boat will be slightly upstream of the other, and this edge is raised very slightly, causing the boat to carve across the pile.

Many who are new to cartwheels find initiating the move in the first place a considerable obstacle, so we'll concentrate on that for a little while.

As the boat carves across the pile, some radical body talk and paddle strokes aid the bow in sinking. You ideally want the bow to sink on edge and the side of the boat to catch the downstream flow. Start the bow sinking by leaning hard forward and raising the downstream knee. This will radically carve the bow down and allow the green water to catch the now upstream edge of the bow. *You ideally want as little green water as possible striking the upstream edge of your boat!* For this reason many people cartwheeling on pourovers initiate well away from the hole's ramp. *Look* at the point where you are planting the bow and keep looking here as long as possible. Lean forward as the bow begins to plunge, so that you do not 'stall' during initiation and wind up bobbing up and down vertically on the hole's pile.

As you were carving across the hole, your paddles should have naturally been held with a light low brace on the hole's pile. At the same time as you lean forward and change edges, transfer this downstream low brace to a hard low brace on the opposite side and push down on this brace. During this part of the cartwheel, the upstream blade (the blade you are low bracing on), serves two purposes: supporting you on edge and pushing the edged bow underwater. Keep this low brace stroke pushing until the boat arcs past vertical, with the stern dropping back into the hole.

As soon as the stern starts to fall back into the hole, transfer the low brace push paddle stroke to a high brace support on the opposite side. Go easy on this. One of the most common mistakes when cartwheeling is pulling too hard on this high brace support and by over rotating, exposing too much surface area of the stern to the green water and pulling yourself out of the hole.

If your bow has plunged at the right place, your high brace support, used as the stern falls, should be held close to the boat's edge and on top of the hole's pile. The whole paddle sequence of a hole cartwheel is the same as that of the eddy line cartwheel, with only two differences:

1. There is usually (but not always) no need to initiate by lifting the bow on a high brace stroke (double pump).
2. Everything happens much, much faster.

Throughout the move it is important to *look* into the hole as long as possible. You should ideally be looking into the hole even after the stern has begun to drop. Then snap your head to look over the opposite shoulder, only when the natural body rotation pulls the hole out of your line of sight.

As soon as the bow arcs past vertical, swing around your body with your paddles and transfer the high brace support to a strong low brace support. This low brace support will aid you to land on edge and will encourage the (edged) bow to purl underwater, thus beginning the whole sequence again for two, three or multiple end cartwheels.

Body

As the boat carves across the hole, edge the boat slightly downstream. This edge combines upstream knee lift and putting weight on your downstream buttock. It is important to

Performer's Top Tip

Cartwheeling's good cos it helps your river running, and when you get nailed in a hole you kind of half know what's going on...

Paul 'Skinny' Jones paddles for Necky and Peak UK. He can be found on a remote river somewhere on planet earth.

look at where you are going to plant the bow. Quickly transfer the edge to an upstream lean, using knee and hips, and lean aggressively forward. This will encourage the bow to purl at the same time that the boat begins to twist onto edge. Keep looking into the hole as long as possible and lean forward throughout the move. As the stern arcs around, the hole will go out of your line of sight. As soon as this happens (and only once the hole is out of line of sight, not before), *snap* your head around to look into the hole over the opposite shoulder. This will encourage the boat's stern to drop into the hole on edge and thus enable further cartwheels. It is important to remember to *lean forward* throughout a cartwheel. By doing so you will make it easier to plunge the bow underwater, and to slow the second point (stern sequence) down. After all, as you saw in earlier exercises, it is quite hard to drop the bow (see popouts), while the stern is relatively easy to plunge into the green water (see back loops).

Boat

While carving across the face of the hole, the boat should be held at a slight ferry glide angle with the upstream edge slightly raised. As the boat begins to drop down the pile and into the green water, transfer this downstream edge to an upstream edge using your knees and hips. It is good practice to catch as little green water on the bow as possible, since too much will cause your cartwheel to be incredibly fast and uncontrolled. Some expert boaters appear to initiate cartwheels while sitting on top of the hole's pile, and without apparently dropping the bow into the ramp at all! At this point the bow will begin to purl underwater, while the transference of edge will have built up enough pre-rotation to twist the boat until

Photo Sequence (overleaf) – Tom Debruslais, Holme Pierrepont- Photos by Pete Astles

Top Left – Initiating with a 'double pump'.
- Boat is held on edge.
- Low brace paddle close to dropped edge provides support and pushes down to encourage bow to 'purl'.
- Note the boat's position is fairly high on the hole's 'pile'.

Middle Left – Low brace support blade pushes down.
- Boater maintains his 'look' into the hole.
- Note that the 'green water' is catching the upstream edge of the boat and arcing it under the pile.

Bottom Left – Low brace 'push' is maintained as the stern begins to drop into the hole.

Performer's Top Tip

When doing cartwheels, always look where you want to be, so as soon as you come around off the second end you flick your head so you're looking in the hole again.

Mark Birkbeck is currently World Junior K1 Freestyle Champion. He paddles for Dagger, Palm, Robson paddles and, of course, himself.

its side is presented to the downstream flow under the pile. This edge is now maintained throughout the cartwheel sequence.

As the bow purls down, the stern arcs across and begins to drop back down into the hole. If the stern is held on sufficient edge, the cartwheel sequence will be smooth and probably continue to third or fourth ends. Too little edge, and excessive green water will pile onto the rear deck, causing a dynamic 'bandit' type exit out of the hole. Too much edge and an 'inverted' loop or a 'blast' often ends the sequence.

Blades

Blade sequences during a cartwheel often vary considerably. Expert boaters may use a vertical draw stroke while on the stern end, to encourage planting the bow into the hole, while many use the blade on the third end to initiate a 'screw up' roll, having caught excessive water on the stern deck. What follows is a brief description of a basic cartwheel blade sequence.

While carving across the hole's pile, the downstream blade should brace slightly on the pile to provide support. As soon as the edge is transferred to an upstream edge, change the brace from a downstream low brace to an upstream low brace; because of the shallow angle of entry into a cartwheel it is both possible, and desirable, to plant this low brace stroke on top of the hole's pile. By doing so you can help drive the bow underwater and, with practice, control your position on the pile so that the upstream edge of the boat catches very little green water.

Photo Sequence (overleaf) - Continued

Top Right - *First transition!* - As the stern begins to drop into the hole, the paddler has changed blades from a low brace push down stroke to a high brace 'pull' on the opposite side of the boat.
   - Note that the stern falls into the hole still on edge.
   - Note that the boater is still looking over his shoulder and into the hole as the stern falls.
Middle Right - Stern lands in the hole (still on edge).
   - Bow arcs upward and starts to rotate upstream.
   - High brace 'pull' stroke is maintained as the bow reaches vertical.
Bottom Right - *Second transition!* - As the bow falls back into the hole the paddler swings the blades across his body so that they drop into the original low brace 'push' position.
   - Note that the paddler is again *looking* into the hole.
   - *Important note* - The bow falls back into the hole *still on edge*... The boater here is going for multiple end cartwheels!

Performer's Top Tip

The idea of a cartwheel is not for the boat to go from one end to the other, it's to get the boat to rotate around your body.

Tom Debruslais has represented Britain in international competitions many times, he can be found in the latest Riot kayak and is recognisable by his distinctive Peak UK kit.

The low brace push down should be maintained until the stern arcs past vertical.

As soon as the boat arcs past vertical and the stern begins to drop back down into the hole, transfer the low brace push to a high brace pull on the opposite side. It is important here to keep this high brace stroke as close as possible to the edged side of the boat. Pushing around and away from the bow will cause the boat to change angle while on its end, creating difficult instability. Go gentle on this high brace pull stroke. An excessively forceful pull will spin the boat and pull you out of the hole.

This high brace pull not only provides support as the bow arcs upwards, but helps push the edged stern down into the green flow. It should be transferred to the original low brace push as soon as the bow starts to drop back into the hole, with the edged boat facing up-stream... Continue as required or at least until your luck runs out!

Common Mistakes

Too much pressure on the high brace pull during the second end sequence will spin the boat. This will result in either a spinning exit on the stern, or in a flat landing facing up-stream, forcing you to re-edge your boat to set up for the third end.

Failing to drop the stern into the hole with sufficient edge will cause excessive water to pile onto the stern. This will cause a dynamic rotating stern exit, from which it is easy to recover with a screw up roll.

Coaching Point

A simple progression from vertical ender to cartwheel depends on discovering the sweet spot of the wave. Once you have discovered and mastered the sweet spot, (the position to place the bow to achieve a consistent end), the progression to cartwheels is not hard.

It is important to ensure that the speed is controlled on entry to the sweet spot. The bigger and steeper the drop in, the greater speed will be generated and therefore the more speed taken off the manoeuvre before a cartwheel can be attempted. The slower the approach the better (you can always add speed).

Controlling this speed is often achieved by using a set up stroke on the side of the cartwheel. This is a reversing stroke and is used to kill the speed generated by the water and gravity. This stroke has two effects:

1. It kills the speed.
2. It will have a degree of turning effect.

For this reason, you will need to set up on the pile of the stopper slightly away from the paddle side, so the stroke draws you onto the line. In other words, you should be aiming to achieve consistent vertical ends from an off set entry to the sweet spot. Often only a few inches of the bow need be covered to generate the end required.

Cartwheel Variations

Since the Ocoee Rodeo World Championships of 1993 the cartwheel has become the favourite move of the freestylist's repertoire; not surprisingly, the cartwheel has been taken out of the holes and onto numerous other river features. The most notable of these cartwheel variations are the 'wavewheel' and the 'hammer'.

Wavewheel

A wavewheel is a cartwheel performed on the back (downstream) side of a standing wave. The moves required are very similar to those required in an eddy line cartwheel so it would be over diligent to go into great detail. However, here are some pointers to help you on your way.

My paddling buddy Darryl Sergisson taught me how to wavewheel using the simple analogy that, instead of driving the bow down as you would in an eddy line cartwheel, you are really *"tripping over the end of the boat"*. Although the actual paddle talk used in a wavewheel is identical to its eddy line variant, there are a few things to bear in mind:

1. Hit the wave with as much forward speed as possible, and time your last forward stroke to *launch* you off the wave's lip.
2. Choose a steep unbroken wave to learn this move; an ideal learning situation is on ocean surf.
3. As you launch over the back of the wave, edge the boat to one side and use the final pull stroke to support this edge as it powers the bow over the wave.
4. As soon as your knees are clear of the peak of the wave, change this pull stroke to a downstream push stroke, just as you would during an eddy line cartwheel. *Timing* at this point is critical. You want to drive the bow down into the water on the back of the wave using a combination of the wave's energy, your speed and edge, and the low brace push. To maximise this combination, the low brace push should be done right on the peak of the wave (you'll know when this happens, since the boat feels almost weightless), throwing the bow down, lifting the stern out of the water and, in effect, over the wave.
5. *Lean forward* as you would do for a flat water or eddy line cartwheel to prevent your boat stalling on the bow, and continue much as you would in a flat water cartwheel. Remember, because you are effectively falling down the back of a wave, this move will be a little quicker than on an eddy line.

Hammer

Recently river running playboaters have taken the cartwheel to the waterfalls. Put simply a hammer is a cartwheel off the lip of a fall. The basic sequence involved is again the same for an eddy line cartwheel, but timing is critical if you are to avoid a life changing event.

Be careful where you choose to try a hammer; a nice clean lip and the absence of a munchy hole at the bottom are favoured. It is a bad idea to try a hammer on a very large waterfall. By its very nature, the outcome of hammer moves tend to be unpredictable at best; there is no point reducing your odds. In an ideal world the first waterfall you hammer off will not only have a clean (unobstructed) entry and landing, but will also have a lip of water pushing further downstream than the lip of rock creating the fall itself. This means that the rock ends in a lip, but the water pushes on a little bit, so that it is unsupported by anything solid and dangerous for a metre or so until it too falls. Be careful though, as such falls tend to be a little back cut. In short *choose your waterfall with care.*

Having chosen your waterfall it's time to bite the bullet. Once you have decided to go for a hammer, there is very little that can be done to compensate for mistakes.

1. Line up for your fall as you would if you were going to simply run the drop (as a saner kayaker normally would). You will probably be going quite fast at this point, although forward paddling will help you initiate the move.

2. About a boat's length (or two depending on your downstream speed) from the lip of the fall, lift the bow of the boat on edge as you would for an eddy line cartwheel, and then *slam* the bow hard on a low brace push stroke. Try and keep calm and fluid at this point; over edging will cause you to capsize as you drop over the fall, and you *really* don't want to run a waterfall upside down do you?

3. If you have chosen a 'good' fall for hammering and timed the move right, your bow should plunge quite easily, since the water is usually both aerated and supported by little more than air, as it flies over the drop. Consequently as you drop over the edge of the fall, you should be standing upright on your edged bow and *looking* down the fall to where you intend to land.

4. Because of the pre-rotation built up as you slammed the bow down, your stern should continue to fall downstream as you drop down the fall. If you desire a 'single end' hammer (fairly similar to a retendo over a waterfall), reach across your boat with the downstream blade (the opposite blade from the one which you initiated with), and push the back of it aggressively into the water cascading down the drop. This should have two effects: twisting your boat while in mid air so that you land flat and facing upstream and, with a little luck, pushing you away from the base of the fall on landing, so that you avoid getting munched by the hole at the base.

If you are extremely brave (or foolhardy) and have chosen an impeccable fall, then you may decide to go for a 'two point' hammer; a full cartwheel off the waterfall. In essence this is reliant on body talk, although your typical cartwheel paddle sequence will help a lot, if only because you have rehearsed the sequence in conjunction with your body talk so often.

As the stern drops away down the fall, you will usually be looking down the fall to your point of landing. As in a conventional cartwheel, your body talk will mean that you are looking over your shoulder, except that, since you are performing the cartwheel downstream, you will be looking downstream rather than upstream into a hole. As soon as the stern has dropped away, *snap* your head around to look over the opposite shoulder. By doing this, your *look will lead the move* and you will (hopefully) throw the hammer into a two point cartwheel. *Good luck… You'll need it!*

Health Warning

The hammer is probably the most dangerous move in any freestyle repertoire. Not only is kayaking off waterfalls extremely dangerous in itself but, by playing as you drop over them, you are to all intents and purposes toying with the River God. Do not be surprised if he is intolerant of your folly, and punishes you with a good whooping in the hole, spinal compression, death or any combination thereof. You have been warned!

7.8 Splitwheels

It wasn't long before 'the move of the nineties' began to be adapted and toyed with. In part, this came about by expert boaters' incredible mastery of the cartwheel, to the point at which unlimited ends became a possibility (if not quite yet a reality). It was also due to frustration at the criticisms that 'rodeo' competitions were becoming little more than cartwheel competitions. By throwing in a 'splitwheel' during a freestyle repertoire, a boater could avoid 'maxing out' (reaching the maximum number of cartwheels possible before the move stopped scoring points in competition), and notch up the more recently introduced 'variety points'.

Prerequisites

Since a splitwheel is based on the cartwheel, it is a good idea to have cartwheels wired before you progress. This of course takes tremendous amounts of practice and I feel that, having got cartwheels sorted so that you can throw multiple ends, you will probably advance onto splitwheels almost naturally. For those having trouble with aspects of splitwheeling a description is included here.

Another move which lends much to splitwheels is the 'one armed bandit' outlined earlier in this book. This is because the second end of a splitwheel reflects the blade and body talk of a one armed bandit well, so go back and practice changing directions in the hole on a single blade.

The Move

A splitwheel starts very much like a cartwheel; the bow purls down, the boat is held on edge so that the upstream side of the boat catches the green water, and support is provided by a low brace stroke close to the edged boat on the hole's pile.

In a traditional cartwheel, as soon as the boat arcs to the vertical, the edge is transferred to the opposite side of the boat and the blade is changed to a high brace on the pile, forcing the stern underwater. The boat's deck faces the same way throughout the move.

In a splitwheel this transitional phase is adapted so that pressure is maintained on the original blade, and the deck of the kayak faces opposite banks between ends, creating an almost gyroscopic effect. It's almost as if the first part of a cartwheel (on the bow) is being linked with a one armed bandit (on the stern), using the same blade to act as support.

Let's look at this in detail. As I stated earlier, the initial phase of a splitwheel is remarkably similar to a cartwheel. Track across the hole with the downstream edge raised slightly, almost as if you are ferry gliding across the pile. Dropping into the hole in this way is very aesthetically pleasing, as the boat's bow drops almost onto the side of the hole pointing across it, and then spins to point upstream, making the boat perform a sort of 'S' shaped sequence on entry.

Drop the upstream edge and lean aggressively forward, encouraging the bow to purl into the green water. This edge transition will encourage the bow to twist so that the upstream edge of the boat catches the green water and the stern begins to arc upward, with the deck almost facing one of the river banks. Remember that you want to catch as little green water on your edged bow as possible.

Throughout this phase the blade is held in a low brace position on the hole's pile. This should provide plenty of support and, by pushing down, should help the bow to dive *just like a cartwheel.* Keep this low bracing blade close to the boat.

Normally in a cartwheel, as soon as the boat arcs to vertical the transitional phase comes into play so that the stern, now on the opposite edge, drops into the trough. In a splitwheel this blade transition does not take place. *However*, the blade pushes down slightly more aggressively and the boat, standing on its bow, twists slightly more than it would in a cartwheel, so that the boater is almost, but not quite, facing downstream.

Throughout this phase, *look* down into the hole. This will encourage your body to:

1. Land back in the hole and retain for an extended ride.
2. Help prevent the boat from twisting on the nose excessively, and pirouetting you out of the hole.

As soon as the twist phase has occurred change the pressure on your blade from a low brace push to a high brace pull. Try and keep your blade on the hole's pile and remember that this action is done *on the same blade throughout*; one of your blades is redundant throughout this move.

This high brace 'pull' will encourage the stern to drop into the hole and help you to maintain stability, as you are keeping the boat held on the same edge at all times (as far as is possible). The pull will force the edged stern into the green water and the bow will arc round to face upstream again; because the bow of the boat is edged as the stern drops back into the hole it will be able to release through the hole's pile with very little resistance.

From this point you have a number of options. Two popular ones are to transfer blades and edges and begin cartwheeling again on the opposite side from which you started, or to keep pressure on the splitwheel blade and either cartwheel on the original edge or continue multiple end splitwheels... *Clever!*

Body

Let's start by considering where to *look* during a splitwheel sequence. As stated many times in this book, thinking about the direction you look during a freestyle move can be the crucial, but subtle, difference between a clean run and a blow out.

Photo Sequence - Martin Tapley, Canolfan Tryweryn

Top Left - Initiate the splitwheel as you would a cartwheel; boat on edge, leaning forward, looking into the hole, pushing down on the low brace.

Bottom Left - The Essential Phase
- Maintain the *look* over the original shoulder
- As the stern begins to drop into the hole change the low brace push stroke into a high brace pull *on the same blade.*
- *Maintain the original edge* as the boat twists, forcing the stern underwater and releasing the bow through the pile.

Right - Either continue splitwheeling or go into a standard cartwheel sequence.

As the boat carves across the hole to set up for the splitwheel, look into the hole's 'pocket' or 'squeeze' at the precise point where you intend to plant the bow. This will usually mean looking slightly over the upstream shoulder as the bow begins to purl down. As the boat purls and you maintain the look, you will be looking almost entirely over this shoulder. This over the shoulder look should be maintained throughout the splitwheel and until you return to a front surfing position.

As in a cartwheel, the boat's initial purl is encouraged by dropping the upstream knee and leaning forward. This will present the upstream side of the boat to the green water. As the boat reaches vertical, twisting on the downstream hip by pushing with your foot on the edged side will aid the boat's twist and help maintain the move's edge. To slow the move down and give you more time to twist, lean slightly back as the bow drops and the stern rises; more time equals more control.

Boat

This move is set up by carving across the hole's pile. Dropping the upstream edge then presents the opposite edge to the green water, and encourages the boat to arc up and around on edge.

Pressure from the low braced blade and body talk twists the boat to face downstream more than it would in a conventional cartwheel. As the stern plunges back into the hole, the original edge should be re-established, allowing the stern to plunge and the bow to slice through the hole's pile, arcing upwards on the original edge in a gyroscopic movement.

Blade

The blade sequence in a splitwheel is less complex than in a cartwheel. This is because there is no blade transition and the whole move happens without the original blade ever leaving the water.

As the bow purls down on edge, a low brace stroke on the pile provides support and pushes down to encourage the purl. This low brace push is exaggerated more than in a cartwheel to encourage the boat to twist on its now vertical nose.

As soon as this happens, the stern should start to plunge and the low brace push should be replaced by a strong high brace pull close to the edged bow, much like in a one armed bandit. It is this high brace pull, edge on the boat and body talk that pushes the stern down and releases the boat's bow from the pile, allowing it to arc back so that it faces upstream.

Common Mistakes

The splitwheel is strange in that it is an easy move to do by accident when learning to cartwheel, but a very hard move to do in a controlled manner when trying for it. Concentrate on looking over the same shoulder throughout the move and not releasing the blade from the surface of the pile.

Back looping off the second end (and out of the hole) is common when learning to splitwheel. This is because the twist tends to kill the edge, and failing to edge the boat as the stern plunges presents a large surface area to the green water rushing under the hole. This in turn causes excessive 'catch' on the rear deck. To remedy this problem practise one armed bandits to the point of frustration. You'll soon come to realise how much water you can allow to pile onto your stern without blowing out of the hole.

7.9 Green Spins and Variations

Just as the cartwheel was the move of the nineties, it looks as though the green spin and its numerous variations will be the move of the new millennium. The green spin first came to the attention of most freestyle devotees following the 1997 Ottawa World Championships. Kayak designer and top paddler Corran Addison had invented a boat so good at green spins that the rules to the competition were reputedly modified at the last minute, causing a protest by the aforementioned designer and hitting the headlines in the kayak press!

A green spin is the art of spinning your boat while surfing a green wave, without resorting to using a pile or break on the wave to assist. As this is a very specialised move, there are some factors to consider before attempting it; these are highlighted in the prerequisites section of this chapter.

Prerequisites

Let's start this section by looking at the kayak techniques and design factors required before you attempt to green spin:

Surfing

The ability to ride a wave, carve across the face, and control your position on the face of the wave are natural 'prereqs'. If you can't surf a wave totally in control, your chances of successfully spinning on a green wave are negligible. When building up to attempt green spins, concentrate on your carving across the wave and controlling where on the face of the wave you surf.

Boat Design

For many years most white water kayaks had what is known as 'displacement' hulls. This means that, if you take a cross section of the hull around the cockpit, the hull will be curved. Consequently, when the boat surfs a wave the shape of the hull creates suction and the boat effectively sticks onto the face of the wave, precluding moves such as the green spin.

In the mid nineties a few boat designers started developing hulls which were capable of spinning on green waves. These boats (the Fury, Whippit, Whiplash) could spin on the green and it wasn't long before other manufacturers produced 'planing hull' boats. Nowadays, 'planing hull' boats are significantly better designed than simply placing a flat hull on an otherwise traditional boat. Some manufacturers put complex grids on their boat's hull, others provide release points toward the bow and stern to allow water to flow from under the boat whilst spinning, making the boat 'looser' on the wave. When green spinning, this concept of 'looseness' on the wave is essential; your boat should skim across the wave's surface rather than sitting down in the wave's face.

Another essential prerequisite is to have your boat 'trimmed' as well as possible. This means that when you sit in your boat on flat water, the boat should sit just as deep in the water on the stern as it does on the bow. This is a major bone of contention since many recent radical boat designs have very little foot room. As a consequence some boaters have resorted to pushing their seats back, making sure that they are able to get into these micro-kayaks, but causing the stern to sink down in the water when on the flat. A badly trimmed boat is very difficult to green spin. Bad trim, no spin.

Performer's Top Tip

Start as high as you can up the wave, you want a bit of speed as you fire down the face, keep the hull of the boat as flat as you can.

Jon 'Pies' Smith is a member of the Eskimo/ Playboater/Werner Pro Team and actually did eat all those pies.

The Move

Start this move as you would with a normal front surf. Get used to the feel of the wave by carving across the face of the wave and back. By doing this quite aggressively, you will soon get to feel the point at which you can maximise your carve and the point at which you will blow off the wave should you carve any further.

By carving aggressively during your front surf, you will also have manoeuvred your boat so that it is sitting quite high on the face of the wave. From this point you should be able to start thinking about a green spin. If you are not yet quite as far up the wave face as you want to be, try putting a couple of slight braking strokes on either side of you and allow these strokes to drag you up the wave.

To change direction while surfing the wave, you must get used to edging your boat upstream so that, in a sideways position on the wave, your boat will be sitting flush with the wave face. In a flat hulled boat this is relatively easy since, when planing, the edges which would normally catch when sideways on and flip you dynamically have risen clear of the water. For this reason do *not* attempt to green spin a 'displacement' hulled boat on a green wave.

There are two stages to a green spin: from the front to back surf and vice versa. We'll begin by looking at front surf into a back surf.

Front To Back Surf

Initiate your spin by sitting as high on the wave face as you can without falling off the back. Lean hard forward to start the boat dropping down the wave and continue this forward lean throughout the move. The forward lean has three effects: it lifts the stern of the boat clear of the water while spinning, it prevents water catching your back deck during the back surf phase of the move, and it launches your boat down the wave, picking up speed for the spin.

As soon as the boat starts to fall down the wave, begin the boat turning with a strong but sharp reverse sweep stroke. As the boat begins to spin, edge the boat using the now downstream knee and hip so that the boat is flush on the wave face. This is the crucial element, as by edging the boat upstream you reduce the amount of resistance the hull of the boat presents to the green water rushing underneath it. Too little edge at this point will cause the downstream edge of the boat to catch the green water and you will carve off the wave, too much edge (upstream lean) and your upstream edge will catch and you will flip upstream... Ouch! You should finish this sequence back surfing the wave with your blade (the one which swept around during the spin) still in the water close to your feet.

Back To Front Surf

Although I describe this sequence as though it is a separate move here, most freestyle boaters barely pause between the phases. By transferring from front to back and again to the front quickly, the boat's spin looks really fluid and the move is smoother. This is because the

The forward lean has lifted the stern clear of the water. - Tim Thomas, Hurley Weir

Photo Sequence - Bleddyn Lloyd, Canolfan Tryweryn

Top Left - The move starts with a front surf.
- Note that the boater has positioned the boat quite high on the wave face.

Bottom Left - Boater leans forward to encourage the boat to drop down the wave face.
- The lean also releases the boat's stern and prevents it dragging as the boat spins.
- *The hull of the boat is as flat as possible on the wave face.*
- Paddler is *pushing* the stern down and around with a stern sweep close to the hips.
- The paddler rotates his head so that he is looking upstream as much as is possible.

Top Right - Into the back surf - The original stern sweep is maintained to continue the spin.

Middle Right -The spin continues and the paddler releases the original blade out of the water and *looks* over his shoulder down the wave.

Bottom Right - The blade is changed and the paddler pushes the bow into a front surf with a forward sweep stroke.
- The paddler is now leaning slightly back to release the bow as it spins.

Performer's Top Tip

When green spinning from front to back, concentrate your gaze down the wave and continue this gaze as long as possible during the move by looking over your up-stream shoulder. By doing this your body will pivot in the opposite direction and your spin will be sweeter! Also, a handy psychological tip for green spinning is to think of the move as though you are throwing your bottom down and around the wave.

Darryl Sergisson is a renowned river runner and playboater with an impressive list of first descents to his name. He loves his Wavesport kayaks.

momentum caused by the transition from front to the back can be continued making the next transition more consistent.

As soon as the transition from front to back surf has finished, make sure that you are stable on the wave. You should be surfing backwards using the drive face of your blades as a rudder, close to your feet. Lean forward; if your stern edges catch it's a dramatic back loop exit for you.

Many boaters begin to spin from back surf to front surf with a slight push stroke close to the boat. This will start the boat dropping backwards down the wave and ensure that you do not drift off the back of the wave during the sequence.

As soon as the boat begins to drop down the wave face, transfer this push stroke to a sharp sweep stroke on the same side, and look over the opposite shoulder. Lean (very slightly) upstream as the boat begins to spin, and kick your legs around using your hips into a front surfing position. Your body weight should be loaded onto the buttock which leads the spin, the one which is upstream as the boat spins around.

Although this may seem quite a complex body talk it really comes quite naturally. All this complexity really just combines to hold the boat flush to the wave while it spins, and if you get that bit wired the rest should flow smoothly.

Body

During a green spin sequence your body controls the boat's angle using your hips and knees. It is important to practice your edging and to get used to the alien sensation of edging upstream while surfing a green wave.

Initiate the green spin sequence by leaning forward while in a front surf position. This will cause the boat to 'fall' down the face of the wave and generate enough speed to prevent the boat falling off the back of the wave during the green spin. Maintain this forward lean as the boat spins into a back surf to prevent the stern's edges catching. Throughout the spin sequence your body weight should be loaded onto your upstream buttock; this will assist in keeping the hull flat to the wave face without unbalancing the boat.

As soon as the boat has swung into a back surf, look over the opposite shoulder and down the wave. As the boat swings back into a front surf, hips and knees aid the edge on the opposite side of the boat and hold the boat flush to the wave face.

Boat

Throughout this whole sequence it is important to hold the (flat) hull of your boat flush to the wave's face. This allows the boat to skid along the wave and to spin with little resistance. Should you fall off the wave during the spin, or carve across the face, it is probable that you have not edged the hull enough and the edges of the box shaped boat are catching too much green water, pulling you downstream.

Initiate the spin by driving the boat down the face of the wave. This will allow the boat to gain momentum as it travels down the wave, and facilitate an easier spin. Even when spinning from a back to front surf, the boat should be falling down the face of the wave.

Blades

During a conventional front surf your paddles will be working as a rudder and controlling the boat's track across the wave. As the boat begins to fall down the wave, a sharp reverse sweep stroke close to your hips will begin the boat's spin and you will quickly find yourself back surfing. Follow this reverse sweep through so that, once you have spun into a back surf, the blade is held close to your feet and is acting as a rudder.

As soon as you reach a back surf position, drop the opposite blade into the water next to your toes and push back on it. It is important to drop this blade quickly so as not to stall the full 360° spin. As soon as you have dropped this blade you will begin to spin back into a front surf. This movement can be speeded up by pulling back on the blade sharply and throwing your legs around into a front surf position.

Common Mistakes

By far the most common mistake in this sequence is failing to edge the boat upstream enough. This presents your downstream edge to the green water and usually creates enough resistance to drag you off the wave. Go back to the eddy and visualise yourself doing the full 360, then try again; the results of prior visualisation are often astounding.

Over edging the boat upstream is a very dangerous mistake to make when attempting this move. By doing this, you present your upstream edge to the green water and the inevitable power flip will at least clear your sinuses for the next attempt.

Don't think of a green spin as though the boat is rotating around the body. Think of it as though the boat is rotating around a point about a foot in front of your body trunk, in this way you will understand Darryl's earlier comment about throwing your bottom down and around the wave.

Green Spin Variations

Grinding Surfs

A grinding surf is when you initiate a green spin, but kill the boat's spinning momentum as soon as the boat is side on, by pulling slightly on the blade that initiated the boat's spin. This works best on faster surf waves and looks extremely cool as you sit edging upstream sideways on to a green wave. (See title photo on page 125).

Shovitts

A shovitt is the green spin version of a splitwheel. It involves spinning into a back surf and then spinning back into a front surf using the same blade. The effect is that of the boat

131

Performer's Top Tip

When initiating all modern wave moves, from spins to aerial blunts, make sure that you throw the move from the top of the wave, just as you begin to slide down the face... Your boat will fly free and clean the move in one.

Pete Astles turned to freestyle after a "wasted childhood as a slalom paddler", and is the owner of Peak UK.

spinning into a back surf and spinning back in the *opposite* direction into a front surf (for example: spinning clockwise into a front surf and then anti-clockwise back to the front). Although very spectacular, it simply involves not releasing your paddle from the water once in a back surf and pulling sharply back on the drive face (which will be near your toes) as soon as you are back surfing. Remember to look over the same shoulder throughout a shovitt, just as you would in a splitwheel.

Cleans

A clean is when you initiate a green spin with a single paddle stroke and spin the full 360° (or more) without using any more paddle strokes. The body and boat talk for a clean has to be almost perfect, so that *no* edges are presented to the green water, and the boat skims 360° with *little* or *no resistance*. A move for the accomplished only.

Ollies and Ollie Oops

Imagine a skate boarder playing at his local skate park. Almost certainly this skate boarder will load all his weight onto the board and then quickly unload it by skipping off the board; because of its natural elasticity, the board will spring into the air momentarily before the gravitational force of the skate boarder comes crashing down upon it... Ollie!

The same thing is quite possible in a kayak. Start the move by leaning hard forward; naturally the bow will drop slightly, but not enough to push you off the wave. As soon as the bow has pushed down under your weight, unload the weight by leaning quickly back. With luck, the right boat, and the right wave, the buoyancy of the boat will skip the bow upward. As soon as it springs up, load the bow again with a hard forward lean; this will unload the stern and it too will spring out of the water. Timed right, and the boat will momentarily skip out of the water and (usually by a matter of inches) clear of the wave altogether... A kayak ollie!

Now combine the ollie with the green spin. Build up your ollies with successive weight shifts fore and aft so that the boat skips a few times, and then very quickly begin the green spin paddle sequence. With luck you'll spin 180° or even 360° (not so much lucky as almost miraculous) with the boat clear of the wave... Ollie oop!

Photo Sequence – Paul 'Skinny' Jones - River Inn, Austria - Photos: Pete Astles / Peak UK
- The paddler here lifts his paddles well clear of the water as he cleans a spin. Doing this in competition will highlight the clean to the judges who may otherwise mistake the clean for an unintentional move.

7.10 Blunts

A blunt is another variation of the green spin but is one which adds variety to a surfing sequence in a spectacular way. A blunt is an elevated green spin, done so that instead of lying flush to the green surf wave, the bow is pushed underwater during the spin. This releases the other end of the boat so that it throws an arc of spray around until it lands cleanly onto the wave.

In many respects the blunt looks like a high velocity cartwheel, performed on a green wave rather than in a hole or on an eddy line. None the less, because waves are not retentive, this move looks particularly skilful.

Prerequisites

You aren't going to perform a blunt in any of the early green spin boats. To do this move, you will have had to invest in a boat with a flat hull and low volume, slicey ends. Most of these boats are fifth generation or later, so you are looking at a new boat!

The prerequisites for a blunt are fairly self evident. You'll have to be comfortable green spinning and generally shredding a surf wave to pieces. You'll also have to be happy loading the front end of your boat, just as you would for a flat water cartwheel.

The Move

Start this move as you would for a conventional green spin. Carve across the face of the wave and get familiar with it. Try and build up to the point at which your carve would pull you off the wave (the release point), and stay *just* short of it.

Start the move by carving aggressively, so that you end up as high as possible on the face of the wave, just as you would for a green spin. A strong forward weight shift will allow the boat to drop down the wave. *Don't* let the boat fall straight down the wave, allow a slight downstream edge which will cause the boat to carve across the wave as it drops. You want to build up as much speed as possible while carving across the wave, so lean forward aggressively to initiate the drop. Keep your blades streamlined so that they slice rather than drag through the water when controlling the direction of carve with a stern rudder. On really good fast waves, you can carve so that the boat points slightly downstream just before you hit the blunt!

You ought to perform your blunt at maximum speed and on the fastest part of the wave. Drop down the wave face and try and hit the wave's 'shoulder' (its fastest and steepest part), facing across the wave. Then, when you hit the shoulder at warp speed... raise the downstream knee so that the boat edges (slightly) upstream, just a bit more than it would for a green spin. As you do this, 'load' the bow by leaning hard forward so that the bow drops underwater. Most boaters aid this bow drop by pushing hard down and at the same time away with a stern rudder on the upstream side of the boat, much as you would in a cartwheel. As you are travelling at such a high speed, it is possible to swing your body out from the boat's centre of gravity so that you hang out from the upstream edge of the boat at this point.

This combined boat edge, body talk and paddle push will force the bow underwater and radically turn it upstream. At the same time, the stern of the boat will release out from the wave and arc around so that, with continued momentum, it lands flat on the wave in a back surfing position. Don't think that the green water rushing under the wave will push the bow downstream or dynamically flip you; you should have enough speed and body talk to overcome its force with ease. Since the speed of the blunt causes a huge build up of momentum, it is quite feasible to go straight from a blunt into a green spin sequence in one smooth movement.

Performer's Top Tip

Look for the maximum speed in everything, if you're looking to do wave moves go as fast as you can...

Paul 'Cheesy' Robertson is two times World Champion in freestyle C1 class, European C1 Champion and has won the British title more times than he can remember. He also does some kayaking in his Pyranha boat and Palm kit.

Body

Prior to attempting your first blunt, it is a good idea to familiarise yourself with your chosen wave. Use your hips and knees to control your carve across the wave.

Once you are high on the wave's face, lean aggressively forward so that the boat drops down the wave. At the same time raise your upstream knee, causing the boat to carve across the face of the wave.

As soon as your feet hit the wave's shoulder, lift the downstream knee (slightly), and lean hard forward so that your body weight combines with the water pushing on the boat's upstream edge to push the bow underwater. Then use a hard hip flick to throw your bum up and around, arcing the stern through the air.

The concept of *looking*, which is the key to conventional cartwheels, is almost redundant during a blunt. The speed build up is so great that looking makes no difference as your stern arcs through the air at Mach 5.

Boat

Carve across the wave until you can carve no further, without carving off the wave itself. Try and get the boat moving as fast as possible, and initiate the move as you hit the fastest part of the wave (preferably at Mach 5 so that the move is more spectacular). Then, in one dynamic movement, drop the upstream edge of the bow and sink it underwater by loading your body weight onto it. The stern will release from the wave face and arc through the air, leaving a vapour trail in its wake and spraying all the others watching enviously from the eddy.

Concentrate on not letting too much water pile onto the deck. Do this by initiating the blunt as the bow turns upstream, so that you don't capsize upstream while the stern arcs... Ouch! The edge of the boat should slice under the water, rather than allow a large surface area to be presented to the green water (and blow you off). If you attempt this move too slowly, say goodbye to the wave as you get blown off.

Blade

While surfing the wave as you build up to your blunt, the blade should be used as a stern rudder. Although this stern rudder helps govern the speed and direction of the carve, it should not 'drag' but 'slice' through the water. As the boat hits the wave's shoulder, this stern rudder should be on the upstream side of the boat and close to the hips, rather than trailing behind you.

As soon as you change edges and lean forward, push down and around with the stern rudder. This helps to force the bow underwater and at the same time pushes the stern (now clear of the wave) around.

Common Mistakes

Over edging while attempting a blunt will cause a dynamic capsize on the face of the wave. Since you have built up considerable momentum, are leaning upstream, and have the blades in a position not conducive to a quick roll, this can be very dangerous (especially for your shoulders). Therefore, try your first few blunts on a wave that has a deep run out, and take your time to recover, or you'll be taking longer to recover from the dislocation.

Photo Sequence – Bleddyn Lloyd, Canolfan Tryweryn

Top - The paddler heads for the wave's shoulder at maximum speed.
- Note the downstream edge of the boat as it carves across the wave face.
- The last second power stroke both lifts the bow slightly and increases the speed.

Middle - On hitting the shoulder the paddler dynamically transfers to his upstream edge.
- Note the radical body talk which accentuates the boat's carve, and that the paddler is leaning hard forward to encourage the bow to slice underwater.
- The paddler leads the move with his paddles and his body rotates to face upstream.
- An assertive stern rudder near the hips on the upstream side helps turn the boat.

Bottom - The boat spins, releasing the stern out of the water in a wide arc and throwing it upstream. Most boaters flatten the stern out so that it lands flat on the wave and reduces the probability of blowing off the wave.

Part Three

Training for Freestyle

Making the most of your abilities as a freestyle paddler and proving those abilities in competition requires hard work. To be the best you can be requires planning as well as talent. In fact planning may well be more important than talent, on the day. This section of the book is about how to make your training sessions count, how to make them as effective as possible.

Effective training and successful competition requires considerable commitment and a willingness to learn. It is not enough to paddle the river aimlessly playing in all the good spots. To get the best from yourself you need to know what you want to do, how you are going to do it and be motivated enough to do it.

Assuming you have read this far, and that winning freestyle competitions is still your aim, you will no doubt appreciate the importance of planning to win. There is an old saying that sums this up perfectly.

"If you fail to prepare you prepare to fail."

So don't forget to plan!

In order to plan effectively you will need to know what aspects of your freestyle paddling need developing. Working on the bits you can already do well, or training hard on skills that are not necessary for competition may be of little use to you. Variety is a wonderful thing to develop, but not if the cost is too great.

To be the best you can be will mean a lot of effort on your part and an understanding of what it takes to become that ultimate athlete. To perform at an optimum level in any sport requires excellence in training for technical ability. However, technical expertise is only part of the equation; often it is how well you handle the pressures, how fit you are and how well you have prepared that will determine whether you win or lose. In freestyle this will often mean training that is not water based.

There are essentially four aspects to training for optimum performance:
1. Technical Ability
2. Tactical Ability
3. Physical Ability
4. Mental Ability

It is how well you understand yourself and your freestyle paddling that will determine which of these aspects you will need to train for. That said, in order to be at your best, you will need to develop each of the four abilities to their optimum level. Some would say that we should view ourselves in terms of four parts that inter-link to form one whole. We should consider ourselves as physical, mental, emotional and spiritual beings, and if we are to be the best we can be, then all four of these parts need to be working in harmony and at full efficiency. It is not the role of this section to consider the spiritual aspect as a separate entity; however, proficiency in the other three sectors may well develop spirituality.

Optimum freestyle paddling is similar to optimum formula one driving. It does not matter how good a technical driver you are; if you enter a formula one race with no idea of tactics, a car that has a body (physical) of an escort and the engine (mind) of a mini, you do not do yourself any favours. Some would say that you even limit your chance of winning!

The development of the technical ability required has already been covered. Part One and Part Two outlined the basics of freestyle, provided some very useful insights into becoming a proficient freestyle paddler and described some exceptional coaching tips and exercises designed to improve your technical performance. This section is about how to develop the other three aspects so that you make the most of your natural and hard earned talents, by highlighting ways to enhance your tactical, physical and psychological abilities.

For organisational ease this section has been split into three chapters. The first discusses the advantages of training preparation and goal setting, the second considers the importance of physical training and the last looks at some ways to train your mind. In considering these three chapters, the mind and body have been written about as two separate entities; this is done for convenience only and is not intended to present the mind and body as mutually exclusive.

Freestyle in canoe sport has developed extremely rapidly and competitors are now sponsored and moving into the realms of professional paddling. As a result competition for the top spot has become even more vigorous and therefore legitimate methods of performance enhancement more important. Whilst this chapter is not intended to be the ultimate in sports training manuals, it is a practical guide to some techniques that you may find useful in your quest to becoming the very best freestyle paddler that you can be.

8 Training and Goal Setting

Training in freestyle is about optimising your performance, whether you are preparing for the rigours of world class competition or your local Sunday league. It is about making sure that you have the right technical, physical and psychological skills plus a good understanding of the tactics that you will need to ensure you paddle at your best.

This chapter covers the basics for training with purpose and proficiency. First the preparation for training is reviewed, then some specific methods for increasing your training effectiveness are covered. Lastly, this chapter describes the process of Goal Setting in detail. The intention is to discuss ways that will help you improve your freestyle training; as such you will find a number of references to skills that are covered in more depth earlier in the book.

8.1 Training Sessions

There are numerous ways to prepare for training sessions and whilst your attitude towards training will be important, it is not everything; you will need to organise yourself as well. In essence, this means that each training session should be well thought out, perhaps even to the extent of developing a routine.

Preparation for Training

To make the most of each training session the following points will be worth considering:
- Set specific achievement goals before each training session.
- Prepare your mind before training to get the most out of each period.
- In training, practice your skills with the maximum attention and effort.
- Use imagery and simulation to mimic actual performance as far as possible.
- Practice distraction, mood and stress control so that they can be applied effectively in competition.

Each of the above points is covered in greater depth later on in this section. For now it is enough to realise that training is different from playing. To be effective you will benefit from having a plan and setting an aim before each training session begins, whether on or off the water. This concept of pre-planning should also be considered before each move. That is, whilst you sit in the eddy waiting for your turn, try thinking about what you want to achieve when it is your go. Imagine yourself carrying out the move you are about to do in as much detail as possible. If you are working on a specific element of that move (e.g. point of entry or head movements), then mentally plan that aspect as clearly as possible.

What to Train for

The next thing to consider in planning your training is what to train for. One way of viewing this is to split your training into four areas: technique, tactics, physical fitness and mental fitness. Technique can be seen as the skills themselves and tactics are those bits that enable you to get the highest score possible (e.g. using the scoring system to its utmost). In a nutshell to be the best you can be requires optimum ability in each of these areas. (Physiological and mental fitness are covered in later chapters).

An example of how you may develop all four aspects could be that in the off season you train for physiological fitness in a gym, three times a week. You develop technical skills by paddling three times a week and your psychological skills five days a week. As the season comes closer you may decide to concentrate on developing a competition run and enhancing specific psychological skills. Thus you decrease your time in the gym and increase your time on the water.

Off Season Training

This is a good time to work on your fitness and specific techniques. Physically, the off season period is good for increasing your strength, and muscular and aerobic stamina. Water sessions can include flat water paddling, perhaps using the fartlek training method, (see physical section) whereby you train with alternate sprints and low intensity work which helps improve the ability of your muscles to keep going in a competition. Strength training is best done in a gym or other facility and off the water.

Technically the off season is useful to refine those tricky skills so that by the time the competition season starts you can focus your energies on winning and not on worrying about your level of ability.

The off season is also the perfect time to master the psychological skills that you have been working on. Using minor competitions to test your skills and develop improvement plans is always worthwhile.

Competition Training

When competitions loom preparation takes on a different perspective, the following provides some pointers to keep in mind:

- Make sure you rest well before a competition; if you do not you could end up overtraining and tire your body and mind. Not ideal when you need to be in top shape.
- Use the pre-performance rituals (e.g. warm ups) and psychological routines (e.g. relaxation) you developed in training so that you start competing in the best frame of mind.
- Stay focused, this is essential for a top performance.
- Remember to learn from your performance, but only once your performance is complete.
- A useful way to develop your own pre-competition training routine is to record everything in your training diary (see later).

Competition preparation helps ensure that you start your performance in a state of flow. Many high level athletes do this by developing routines that help them to focus their minds on the task in hand and block out distractions. You should experiment with developing a ritual that covers all the points of preparation that you consider important. By practising this ritual and keeping it standard in training, it will become automatic and complete when you enter a competition.

In essence, anything that ensures that you enter a competitive situation in the ideal state of mind and body and that helps you give an excellent performance, must be worthwhile.

Overtraining

One last thing to be aware of is that it is possible to overtrain. Overtraining will drain your mind and body resulting in decreased performance. So don't push yourself too hard. Remember to have fun!

Remember to have fun! - A young 'Pies' - Photo: Bob Timms

Summary

Training should include developing the physical, technical, tactical and psychological skills required to perform at your best in competition. Competition is not the ideal time to try out new, unpractised moves. Each session, whether in the gym or on the water, should be planned before the session starts.

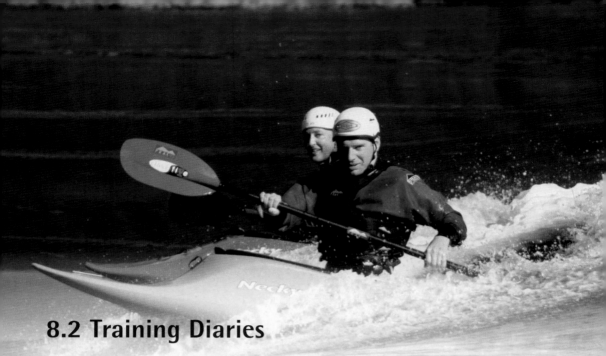

8.2 Training Diaries

A training diary will help you record and plan your training and enhance your ability to set routines that work for you. You can help yourself to effectively apply sports science techniques by getting into the habit of using a training diary before and after every training session and performance.

Developing the Diary *(see fig. 1)*

One way of developing your own diary is to start with a large A4 diary and write in all the competition dates that are relevant to you. Then write in any other important dates (e.g. training camps etc.). It is probably best to write these on the top of the page because the rest of the page will be where you write the main body of your training and performance details.

Ideally you will need a section to cover what you are going to do in this session, (whether in the gym, on dry land, or on the water) and a section that covers what actually happened (physically, technically, tactically and psychologically). It would also be a good idea to include a section that can be used for learning points.

In essence then, block each page into sections for:

Entries Before the Session:

Goals - enter the main goals to be achieved in the training session or performance here. Base the setting of goals on notes from previous pages of the diary.

Entries After the Session:

Achievements - Write down the goals that you have achieved and those that you have not.
Quality of Session - Note your assessment of the quality of the session. This may be a combination of weather and water conditions or linked to a general feeling that the session was worthwhile or unsuccessful. Include any times or scores you achieved.
Mindset - Record your mood, susceptibility to distraction, feelings of stress, and feelings of focus/flow etc.. If you score these they will make more sense in the future. Note why you think you felt the way you did.

Date: Special Notes:
Today's Goals: *(e.g. technical, tactical, physical, psychological)* **1.** **2.** **3.** **4.**
Main Body
1. *(note both achievements and non achievements and why they were or were not achieved)*
2.
3.
4.
Session Quality *(general conditions or thoughts)*
Mindset *(how you felt)*
Learning Points *(to take through to the next session)*

Fig. 1.   An example of a training diary sheet.

Learning Points - Note points to develop here and suggestions for future improvements or possible future goals.

Keeping a Diary

As you get used to using the diary you will find it will help in many ways. Keeping a diary will help focus your attention before a session on what you need to achieve, thus helping ensure that training sessions and performances are always useful for improvement of skills. It will help you keep track of the achievement of goals, and feed information back into the setting of new goals. This will also help to build your confidence as you can easily see what you have achieved.

You will find that a diary will help isolate areas that need improvement so that you can plan to work on them. The information collected will help you track improvements over time so that you can see how you are developing.

It will help you to see and analyse how psychological factors affect your performance and flow, which will help you to develop and apply appropriate management programmes.

Summary

If used properly the training diary will soon become an indispensable tool. You will soon start to wonder how you ever coped without one. Your diary will provide you with essential records and help you develop appropriate focus for competition and training.

8.3 Warm Up and Cool Down

The importance of the warm up and cool down are all too often misunderstood. They both have implications for physical preparation, injury prevention, psychological preparation, and performance enhancement. Those strange contortions that are often seen on the side of the river do have a purpose.

The Warm Up

The importance of a warm up session will be different for each individual and will depend on your own personal style. However there are a few consistent elements to warming up that should be considered. These will help you maximise the benefits and ensure you do not injure yourself.

Benefits in Warming Up

Physically, the benefits are numerous. Warming up will help raise your body temperature and increase the body's basic ability to function optimally. Thus, by the time you are ready for action your body is functioning at its maximum capacity. A cold body is rather like a cold engine, it takes time to get warm and therefore function at its optimum capacity. The exercises you carry out in your warm up will help prevent injury. In any tough activity, especially one that is carried out in cold water, if you put your muscles under strain you maximise your chances of serious injury. Warming the body and mobilising it will help reduce this risk.

Psychologically the warm up is a perfect opportunity to practice the routines you developed in the off season. If you like to listen to music to relax yourself or psyche yourself up then put your headphones on now. The warm up is also a good time to carry out those focus exercises. The warm up can also be used as a psychological thermometer, whereby you take note of how you feel during the exercises and apply adjustments as you go. For example, you may have had a heavy night or feel tired because you have driven for hours; as you go through your warm up you may realise that you are feeling a little too relaxed, more so than usual. To counteract this, you may decide that your on water section will include a few bursts of upstream paddling to psyche up, or perhaps you could use that visualisation technique you developed in the off season. Whatever you use, whether it be techniques designed for psyching up or relaxing or to enhance your motivation to win, this initial warm up period is ideal for mental preparation.

Technically and tactically the warm up period can be used to visualise your performance routine (which you should have by now) or specific moves. The use of basic 'on the water' skills can also help boost your confidence.

The Warm Up Routine

1. Make sure you warm your body before trying any joint or muscle routine. A good way to do this would be to take a brisk walk until your heart is starting to pump hard and your body feels warm. You will probably find that this will take five to ten minutes depending on your level of fitness and how cold the day is. The best time to do this is once you have changed into your paddling gear and are ready to get on the water.

2. Mobilise your joints by moving them through their range of motion. Basically, this means slow hip rotation, shoulder rotation, wrist rotation, finger wiggles and the like, so that the joints are ready for action. You will probably find that your best results occur when your whole body is effectively mobilised. Even the condition of your ankles will affect your ability to paddle well. This will probably take you about five to ten minutes to do well.

3. Stretch those muscles just to let them know that they are about to be used. This is not the time to develop flexibility, so all you need to do is hold a position that feels comfortable (see Chapter 9.3) for about ten to fifteen seconds. It is probably best to do this section on the river bank because you will need to stretch your whole body from ankles to fingers. This section will last about ten to fifteen minutes.

4. Do a whole body warm up, just to get your body back up to working temperature. You could repeat no. 1, probably for five minutes.

5. Get on the water. Once you are on the water it is still a good idea to do some specific boat based mobilisation work for a few minutes. If nothing else this will loosen up your specific paddling muscles and get your body used to the range of motion it will soon need to work within. This will probably only last a few minutes.

6. Warm up those skills, so that your basic skills are well and truly fixed in your mind and body. Depending on your personal choice this could mean ferry gliding, surfing or two point cartwheels. The trick is to make sure that the skills you use in this section are well within your capabilities. This section will take as long as you feel necessary but will usually last about five to ten minutes.

Your total warm up will take between thirty and fifty minutes, depending on your state of readiness, the temperature and what you would like to include.

To Routine or Not to Routine

The warm up has a number of benefits as we have just seen. This section is about how we can maximise those benefits. A deliberate well planned warm up will be useful as a routine that can optimise readiness. In essence the routine works because you are using the same exercises in the same order in training and in practice. Hence it is a useful way to ensure that you develop the same state of readiness in your competitions as you do in your training. The disadvantages in having a routine that is too prescriptive is that if something goes wrong with your routine then that may affect your thoughts and potentially your performance.

A warm up that has plenty of variety and no structure may help strengthen your ability to cope with anything. The advantages of this type of warm up are, amongst many, that you will develop the skills required to focus under most distracting conditions and whatever the situation throws at you. The down side may be that you will miss some important aspect of your pre-performance preparations and become injured or perform badly.

Probably a good way to compromise and maximise your warm up is to develop a routine that has space for variety. For example, you may decide to stick to the sections noted above and have a whole string of stretches, mobility exercises, on the water exercise etc. that you can draw on as required. That way, you still cover all the sections, have time for psychological preparation but can choose the specific exercises you use depending on your feelings at the time. The warm up can then be adjusted for the conditions, your mood or even the site you are paddling on.

Cool Down

After exercise or even after a heavy run, the body needs to keep ticking over. This may mean that after your run you continue to paddle around for a few minutes, instead of sitting in the eddy, whilst preparing for your next run. Once the competition or training session is finished the cool down should really include a few more specific exercises. It is probably a good idea to loosen the body before it starts to get cold, perhaps even carrying out the same routine that you did as a warm up. In essence, the cool down section will help ensure that your body gets over the effects of activity as efficiently as possible. The cool down has implications in reducing stiffness as well as ensuring your blood supply is working properly.

Summary

The warm up and cool down sessions are an essential part of your training and competition procedures, not just because you will prevent injury but also because of the knock on effects that will benefit your psychological, physical, tactical and technical abilities. If used effectively they can make the difference between competing or training at your very best and just getting by.

8.4 Goal Setting

The concept of goal setting is one that is commonly used by successful people in business as well as in sport. In essence, goals help plan, define, and develop the resources needed to realise any dream. If you use goal setting proficiently you will be able to define what is important to you and what is merely a distraction. Goal setting will help you with your long term aims and enhance your motivation to achieve them. As a technique it can be very powerful, providing the principles are understood.

Principles of Goal Setting

In essence, goals are either linked to an *end result* or to the *process* of getting that end result. For example if your *end result* was to win the next freestyle competition, the *process* could be to complete a pre-set series of moves. The major difference between the two is that the first (end result) relies on you beating others and is therefore outside of your personal control, whereas the second (the process), is within your personal control. The very fact that an individual is in control of a process goal means that setting goals that are process oriented seems to work better than goals that are results oriented.

If you base your goals on personal performance targets or skills to be acquired, you can keep control over the achievement of your goals and draw satisfaction from them. If however you concentrate on end result goals, you will have no control over their achievement. For example, you might have the thrill of achieving the best run of your career, but, because of a poor judging decision, you get placed last. If you had set an end result goal of being first, you would have failed and probably felt defeated. If, however, you set a process goal of achieving your predetermined routine, then you will have achieved the goal and would be able to draw satisfaction and self-confidence from its achievement.

Today's environment of sponsorship provides another good example of the difficulties associated with setting end result goals. These goals are usually linked to the rewards of winning (e.g. financial gain or personal recognition). To begin with these factors will be highly motivating, however, as they are achieved, the feeling of excitement in winning at the same level reduces and the pressure to succeed increases. In essence, you could become progressively less motivated and feel more under pressure.

Setting process goals reduces this risk and enables you to draw incredible satisfaction from reaching your goal and achieving what you set out to achieve.

Effective Goal Setting

The methods used to define and set goals are numerous and acronyms such as SMART or POWER are often used as pointers.

In this case, POWER stands for:

Positive - State goals and outcomes in positive terms.

Outcome - What you want to achieve.

What specifically - Specify time and details. What it will feel like, look like, sound like?

Ecological - What personal cost is associated with achieving the goal?

Realistic - Is your goal realistic?

SMART stands for:

Specific - Be specific about what you want to achieve.

Measurable - Define how you will know you have achieved it.

Achievable - Can you reach that goal?

Realistic - Is it based on factual and relevant information?

Timed - Write down when you wish to achieve it by .

These acronyms can be very useful reminders of the principles required to set and achieve appropriate goals. For goals to be effective a number of considerations are necessary.

Positive

It is important to frame your goals in a positive manner and to view the attainment of the goals as desirable. A goal should be something you want to achieve, not something you want to get away from, it is best to 'want to win' as opposed to 'don't want to lose'. As an illustration of the importance of this point, I do not want you to think of a great big pink and hairy elephant. My guess is that you probably did think of a great big pink and hairy elephant; your imagination may even have gone one step further and seen the elephant dance or heard it trumpet. Now if I say that, by the end of this sentence, I would like you to stop thinking of that great big pink and hairy elephant, you will probably still be thinking of it. The point is that if we concentrate on what we do not want it often fills our subconscious thoughts.

Specific and Measurable

Goals should be specific and measurable, for example front surfing a wave for five seconds as compared to doing the best you can. There should be a long term aim that can be broken down into shorter term steps.

Achievable and Challenging

A goal should provide a challenge that is achievable, not too easy or too difficult. Setting goals at the correct level is a skill that is acquired by practice. You should set goals so that they are slightly out of your immediate grasp, but not so far that there is no hope of achieving them; no one will put serious effort into achieving a goal that they believe is unrealistic.

However, just because you believe that a goal is unrealistic it does not mean that it is; you need to be objective and honest. Personal factors such as tiredness, injury, stage in the season and so on should be taken into account when setting goals.

Prioritise

Set priorities; when you first assess your goals you may well find that you have too many to concentrate on. Prioritising them helps define their importance and makes them easier to attain.

Written Down and Timed

Goals should be given a time in which to be completed and written down.

Whilst it is important to consider these points it is also important to remain realistic in your desire to improve. Therefore, you should continually revisit your goals and check how they meet with your future desires.

"Goal setting is a tool designed to help an athlete, not to be used as a tool to punish."

One of the most appropriate ways to set goals is with assistance from a significant other, for example your coach or training partner. Together you can define the desired outcomes, set the appropriate priorities, plan the stepping stones and set realistic time frames.

Stages

There are a number of stages to go through when setting goals, some of which are considered below:

1. Write down all your desired outcomes.
2. Select which are most important.
3. Apply a measuring criterion or score to each outcome (if required).
4. Write down where you are now.
5. Score where you are now (if required).
6. Plan stepping stones and times – be realistic.
7. Assess resources needed to successfully attain stepping stones.
8. Revisit, learn and modify on a regular basis.

It is essential to be honest about how important a desired outcome is as it will be difficult to keep to the plan if the outcome is not important. It is also essential to be realistic about the need for a desired outcome, for instance you may like the stern dip and wish to keep practising it, but will it help you achieve your desired outcome?

1. Write down all your desired outcomes.

You should consider all aspects of your life, as some aspects may present conflicts in your freestyle career and therefore need clarification. For example, is it realistic to want to train six days a week when you have to work or prepare for exams, or need to finish a project or assignment?

2. Select which are most important.

Each goal should be given an importance rating. For example very important, important, mediocre importance, not so important, not relevant. Where you have several goals, give each a priority. This helps you to avoid feeling overwhelmed by too many goals, and also helps direct your attention to the most important ones. The goals that you consider the most important will become your long term ones.

3. Score each outcome.

Many goals have an easily defined set of evidence criteria and may not need further scoring. For example, surfing a wave for five seconds can be easily measured and therefore improvements easily recognised. Some skills (e.g. improving stroke efficiency) are harder to define, and will need a score system. By defining the desired outcome and then applying a score (e.g. 1 – 10), it is possible to create a measure of what success is and therefore note any developments. In this case you will need to be very specific in defining what the optimum is (e.g. blade 70% in the water is equal to a score of 10) and where your present level of skill is so that you can measure any improvements.

4. Write down where you are now.

In this section you should define your current situation as compared to your desired outcome. When setting your competitive goals, it is worth considering what your life goals are, so that you can further assess your commitment to the sport in the context of your career, relationships, ongoing education, and so forth.

5. Score where you are now.

If the skill requires a score system then you should use the same system to note where your current level of skill is.

6. Plan stepping stones and times.

By now you should have a list of your important (long term) goals, a measure of success (e.g. 8) an idea of your current situation and score (e.g. 4). This stage is where a plan is created to bridge the gap between present state and desired state. This is also the stage that timelines (setting of time criteria) are applied.

Write goals down to avoid confusion and give them more force. If a goal is too large, then it can seem as though you are not making progress towards it. Breaking them down into medium term goals gives more opportunities for success. You can break them down even further when setting your short term or daily goals.

7. Assess the resources needed.

This is where you work out how to attain each step and eventually the ultimate goal. You may find that you need assistance from your coach or training partner to complete this section. Resources may well include technical coaching or mental skills training.

8. Learn from the experience.

If you failed to reach your goal, then learn from the experience. For example, you may decide that you didn't try hard enough, or that an aspect of your technique was faulty and needs to be adjusted, or that the goal you set was unrealistic. Use this information to adjust the goal if it was set too high, or to set new goals, if appropriate. Using information like this turns everything into a positive learning experience. Even failing to meet a goal is a step forward towards your long term aim. Remember, the very fact you tried something, even if it does not work, may spark off ideas that you could find useful in the future.

If you have achieved your goal, then use the information to develop your next goals. For example if the goal was easily achieved, make your next goals harder or if the goal took too long to achieve, make the next goals a little easier. If you learn something that would lead you to change goals still outstanding, then do so.

. If whilst working towards one of your goals, you notice a skill deficit, set goals to fix this. Remember, goals are a tool that you use to direct and motivate yourself, so as you develop and grow you will need to adjust them regularly to reflect this growth. If goals no longer hold an attraction, let them go.

Goal Planning Sheet for Medium Term Goals

	End Result	Time Line	Process 1	Score	Process 2	Score
Long Term Aim	*Win competition*	*June, next year*				
Medium Term	*Win competition (Dec. 15th)*					
		Dec. 10th	*10 sec. to paddle 20 metres*			
		Oct. 10th	*12 seconds*			
		Aug. 10th	*14 seconds*			
Current Date		*June 10th*	*16 seconds*			

Fig. 1   Example of a Goal Planning Sheet

"Goal setting is your servant, not your master."

The process should bring you feelings of real pleasure, satisfaction and achievement.

The Example *(see fig.1)*

As a result of completing stage 1 and 2 you have determined that your long term aim is to win an important competition next June, a year away. You have also learned that forward paddling is the skill that needs developing. In fact, by timing your runs to date, you have realised that one third of your competition run time is spent paddling forward. To have a good chance of realising your long term aim you would need to reduce your twenty metre forward sprint time from sixteen seconds to ten seconds and thus increase the amount of time on the wave.

In this case the desired outcome is to take ten seconds to cover twenty metres. This outcome is easily recorded and measured so you do not need to apply a score to it. You are aware that the distance could be covered in a shorter time, eventually, but for now you are being realistic and ten seconds is realistic.

You know your current situation, i.e. twenty metres in sixteen seconds.

The next stage is to plan steps and timelines. In this case you have determined that your ultimate goal of twenty metres in ten seconds should be reached by the next competition, six months away, hence you know the final date and time. The difference between the two times is six seconds and therefore, as luck would have it, you have determined that each step of one second will take one month to attain. You can now set times and dates for monitoring this and write them in your training diary.

Now you are ready to determine what resources are required to complete each step successfully. On reflection you have decided that your fitness is fine but your technique needs some work. With your coach or training partner you determine that Monday, Wednesday and Thursday evening will be forward paddling night. These sessions will last two hours from seven till nine pm. Monday night will be with your coach and Wednesday and Thursday will be practising Monday's skills. Of course these sessions also need to be run using short term goals. With your coach or training partner's help, you can work out how to improve your times. It may be that the aspects of your technique that need improving also need careful assessment and a scoring system applied to define your outcome and current situation (see fig. 2). If so do it.

Each week and month you assess your performance against the criteria you set, and reassess the goal. For example it may well be that you meet your goal in the first month. If so, take the time to enjoy the sense of satisfaction. Appreciate the implications of the goal achievement, and observe the progress you have made towards other goals. Enjoy the feelings that go with goal achievement and learn from them.

This section has outlined an example of the process whereby the measurement criteria was relatively straightforward. However, it is important to remember that some elements are less easily measured and require more precise use of a scoring system.

Forward Paddling (Sprint): *(present profile - June 10th)*										
Paddle 20 metres in 16 seconds										
Score	1	2	3	4	5	6	7	8	9	10
Overall Current Score					X					
Arm speed				X						
Paddle angle					X					
Amount of paddle in water			X							
Shoulder use			X							
Upper back use							X			
Use of feet						X				

Fig. 2a   Goal Scoring Sheet (present profile)

Forward Paddling (Sprint): *(desired profile - December 10th)*										
Paddle 20 metres in 10 seconds										
Score	1	2	3	4	5	6	7	8	9	10
Overall Desired Score								X		
Arm speed										X
Paddle angle									X	
Amount of paddle in water								X		
Shoulder use									X	
Upper back use								X		
Use of feet										X

Fig. 2b   Goal Scoring Sheet (desired profile)

Summary

Goal setting is probably the most important skill to master. The processes will be important in developing all aspects of your freestyle performance. Like any journey, if you do not know where you are going, how to get there or where you are starting from, the chances are you will never reach your destination.

So remember, goal setting is important in:

- Deciding how committed you are to your sport
- Deciding what is important for you to achieve, and what is irrelevant
- Motivating yourself to achieve
- Building your self-confidence

To be effective in setting goals you will also need to:

- Phrase them positively
- Define them precisely
- Prioritise multiple goals
- Write them down
- Keep them manageable; not too hard, not too easy
- Set process goals

Remember:

Failing to meet your goal is useful feedback and can be used to improve technique and long term success, providing you learn from the experience and use the information to develop your training programme.

Enjoy the achievement of reaching your goals. You should also learn from this experience and use the information to develop your training.

You can use goal setting to improve technique, competition tactics, mental skills and body conditioning.

As a final point, if you do not already set goals, or if you have not yet focused on your life goals, now is a great time to start!

8.5 Conclusion

This chapter has considered the complex matter of training, and how to effectively develop so that you perform at your best. To begin with, training sessions were examined and important points were noted. Observations were made on the importance of knowing what to train for and how to manage your on and off season training. Next the notion of written and recorded training details were defined. In this section we looked at training diaries and how to develop and keep them. Thirdly the necessity of the warm up and cool down session was examined. The conclusion being that both are important and knowing how to carry out both effectively is essential. Lastly, goal setting was explained, and the principles and stages of the processes were detailed.

Essentially training is about optimising your potential. How you plan your training will affect your ability to do this. It is important to know:

- What you want
- How you are going to get it
- How you will know when you have got it
- The plan which will enable you to get it

It is possible to be very effective without training, if you have the talent, but if you want to ensure you really are able to be the very best you can be, then training effectively is essential.

Like any skill, training effectively will take time to master and will require a conscious effort on your part to learn the necessary skills.

"Your efforts will be their own reward."

Your efforts will be their own reward, especially as you develop your skills and start to realise your dreams.

9 The Body

Physical fitness for freestyle involves developing your strength, stamina and speed, as well as ensuring that your body is running on optimum fuel. It is all too easy to forget this last aspect or to assume that as long as we are not hungry all is well. Unfortunately this is not the case.

Training to make the most of your physical fitness involves a great deal of thought and planning. It is quite normal for athletes to have diaries that are solely used for keeping track of their nutritional needs or physical fitness. Many universities and fitness centres have specialist equipment that can assess the level of fitness you currently have and help you design a physical fitness routine that will suit your needs.

Physical fitness is also very sport specific. Using a training routine that a marathon paddler or Olympic weightlifter uses for their sport may actually interfere with the development of optimum ability in freestyle. Therefore it is important to assess what type of fitness is needed in your sport. Freestyle involves a considerable amount of flexibility, paddling and body speed, static strength, muscular endurance and, to a lesser degree, a specific type of general stamina. Training for optimum physical performance in freestyle will mean that you train your body to develop your weak points and enhance your stronger points, within the freestyle framework.

This chapter starts by considering a routine for developing strength, then moves on to discuss ways of developing muscular and aerobic stamina. Next flexibility is considered, and finally some important points about nutrition are examined. The intention is to pinpoint some crucial factors in each of these sectors that will help you develop the physical fitness required to get the best out of your freestyle paddling.

As a last and very important point, if you have any doubts about your readiness for physical exercise you should check with your doctor or your local fitness experts.

9.1 Strength

One aspect of fitness is the development of strength. Strength is the ability to apply force and is required in static movements (for example when riding sideways in a stopper), explosive movements (such as a burst for the eddyline) and dynamically (the ability to maintain effort when getting on a wave). As can be seen by these examples there are benefits attached to maximising your strength as a paddler.

The type of exercise that you carry out will depend entirely on which part of your body requires development and what type of development is required. To ensure that you maximise your personal potential it is always best to consult a fitness coach who will be able to guide you through a programme designed for your needs and monitor your progress with you. Whilst it is possible to effectively develop strength by using your own body weight in specific ways, one of the most efficient training methods involves weights. These can be free (dumb-bells, etc.), or machine based. Most sports centres will have the facilities you require, however equipment can be purchased for home use as well. One thing that should be pointed out is that weight training is beneficial for women and men.

Care should be taken when using any kind of strength training programme so as not to create injury or excess stress on the body. For this reason it is important to maintain excellent form and not to attempt weights that mean technique is lost.

How to Use Weights

When developing strength the body adapts to the forces placed on it. That is, muscles, nerves and bones will be affected positively by strength training. For the younger readers it is therefore very important that you seek expert help from your local gym, (training with weights before your body is sufficiently developed can lead to long term damage). In fact anyone unsure about their own situation should check with their doctor first.

Assuming all the checks have been carried out and you are now happy to proceed I have outlined a programme to develop all round conditioning and help you paddle at a higher level.

This programme should really be carried out three days a week and with a day's rest between each training day.

A few things to consider before trying it out. The weights to be used will be different for everybody. I suggest that you attempt low weights and slowly increase the weights until you find a weight that enables you to complete the training below without straining yourself. Remember, complete all exercises through the full range of motion.

A little tip - focus your attention on the muscle area doing the exercise and specifically on ensuring that the action is carried out slowly and in control.

Some weight training terms:

Repetitions - the number of times an exercise is carried out

Set - a series of repetitions

The examples concentrate on training in a gym but can be adapted for home use.

The routine

Exercise	Repetitions	Sets
Warm up		
Bench Press	8-10	3
Stomach Crunches	15-20	3
One Armed Row	8-10	3 (each arm)
Seated Twist	15-20	3
Shoulder Press	8-10	3
Leg Raises	15-20	3
Leg Curl	8-10	3
Leg Press	8-10	3
Back Extension	8-10	3
Cool Down		

Bench Press

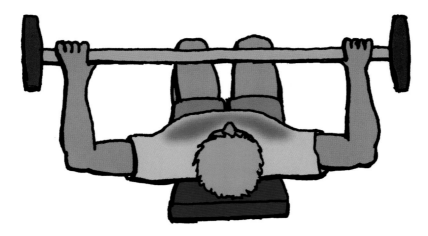

Bench Press (See drawing on previous page)

The bench press develops the chest area.

Lie flat on a bench with your feet positioned for balance (not force). Grip the bar so that your hands are positioned slightly wider than your chest. Ideally your forearms should point straight up when the bar is lowered to the chest. Next, lift the bar from the rest position then straighten your arms to full length. Then lower the bar slowly until it touches your chest. Repeat.

(For home use, substitute the press up, and raise your legs on to a chair or bed for extra difficulty).

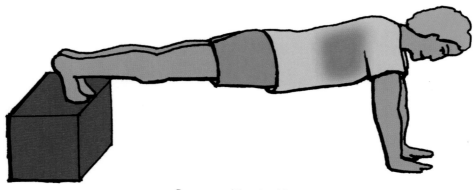

Press up with raised legs

Stomach Crunches

Develops the front of the stomach.

Lie flat on your back with your legs resting on a bench or chair. Place your hands to the side of your head, (do not use them to pull your head up). Concentrate on your stomach area and gently curl the upper body as high as it will go. Gently lower and repeat.

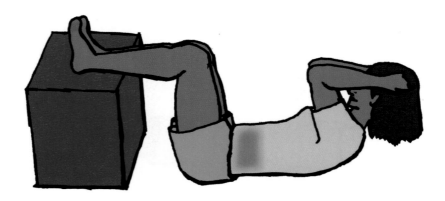

One Armed Row

Develops the upper and mid back.

Bend forward from the waist, keeping your back straight, and support your body by placing one arm (and possibly leg) on a bench or chair. With the other arm take hold of the dumb-bell and pull it upward to the chest, slowly, then lower and repeat.

Seated Twist

Develops the side of the stomach.

Sit on the end of a bench or seat, feet flat on the floor. Take a bar or broom handle and hold it across the back of your neck, let it rest on your shoulders. Keep your pelvis still and your head facing forward. Gently twist your torso towards the left and then the right. Feel the muscles tense on each side. Repeat.

Shoulder Press

Develops the shoulders.

Best done sitting. Hold bar across the front of the chest with arms slightly wider than shoulder width apart. Gently push the bar straight up and lower it again. Make sure the back is kept straight.

Leg Raises

Develops lower stomach.

Can be done lying down or hanging from a bar. Gently raise your slightly extended legs to 90° and lower. Repeat. If lying down ensure that your back is kept flat on the floor.

Leg Curl

Develops the back of the legs.

Lie face down on the leg curl bench and hook your ankles under the mechanism. Raise your feet, keeping your upper legs flat on the bench and bent at the knees as far as possible. Gently lower. Repeat.

(To do this at home you will need to attach ankle weights to one leg. Then, support yourself against a door frame or similar and bend the leg).

Leg Press (squats)

Develops the front legs.

Hold the barbell across the top of your back, behind your neck, with your feet a comfortable width apart, about shoulder distance. Keep your back straight and bend your knees and lower your upper body so that your thighs are slightly lower than parallel to the floor. Straighten your legs. Repeat.

Back Extension

Develops the lower back.

This one requires a specialist bench. Lie across the bench facing the floor, with feet hooked under the rear support. Bend forward so that your upper body points to the ground. Straighten up to parallel (do not go further). Repeat.

Summary

Strength is a vital part of freestyle excellence, and training to maximise your potential will be of considerable benefit. The routine provided here will not suit everybody, so adapt it to your own needs. It is also possible to carry out the exercises a little faster than hinted at, this will help increase your movement speed. If you do exercise for speed it is still essential to maintain good body posture and technique.

9.2 Stamina

Stamina or endurance has far reaching effects in any physical activity. It is the ability of the body to keep on going for a prolonged period without fatigue. Endurance can be seen in terms of muscular endurance (the local effect), whereby a muscle group can keep working without performance impairment, or general endurance, which describes the body's ability to efficiently transport oxygen, and includes the heart and lungs. In kayaking, a paddler with good endurance will be able to keep going for longer, make less mistakes, and have less chance of getting injured.

This type of exercise is probably the easiest to explain as most people will have carried out endurance exercise at some stage in their lives. This is the type of exercise that is developed through activities such as running, cycling and swimming.

To develop stamina effectively and specifically for freestyle it is best to train in a similar way to freestyle. Swimming therefore would provide a good endurance exercise as would flat water paddling. It is also possible to purchase machines that simulate the basic paddling action.

One other consideration is that cross training or using other techniques can be useful in that it improves basic fitness and also allows for variety, which may help you to stay motivated.

Types of Training

First a little bit about the theory behind endurance training. It is possible to train for endurance in different ways.

Interval Training

Interval training includes short spurts of hard work with brief periods of rest or reduced activity. The hard work section varies in duration from about thirty seconds to five or six minutes and the rest or light exercise periods vary in line with that required to carry out the periods of hard work. To develop this type of exercise you can speed up the hard work periods or shorten the light exercise periods, or lengthen the period of hard exercise. The heart should be beating at a rate within your heart rate zone (Page 169).

Circuit Training

Circuit training uses a variety of stations each with an exercise to carry out. The athlete does each exercise in turn. Generally each station has an exercise that works a different part of the body such that the heart rate is kept within the training zone and all body parts are used. It is possible to set this type of exercise up at home or join a gym.

Long Slow Distance

Long slow distance is when the athlete carries out low intensity training for a long period of time. Generally this type of exercise is carried out at about 60-70% maximum heart rate.

Pyramid Training

Pyramid training can be used to develop speed and endurance for the longer distance sports. In essence the athlete picks set distances or times and at each pre-set point increases intensity. For example you can start off gently then at a pre-set point run or swim harder then at another pre-set point harder still, eventually you will be running flat out. At the next pre-set point you drop back to steady exercise, and then repeat the cycle.

Fartlek Training

Fartlek training involves intensity variation. In effect the exercise is carried out with spontaneous bursts of hard work interspersed with periods of lighter work. Once again, it is possible to develop with this exercise through increasing the amount of hard work, decreasing the rest period or increasing the intensity of hard work.

There are many other methods of training, such as aerobic classes and step classes should you wish to develop this aspect of your training and many books written on the subject.

"Remember to always warm up before exercise and cool down after exercise."

The best type of exercise is the one that you feel most comfortable with. In general all the above types of training should be carried out within your heart rate zone whereby flat out exercise relates to about 85% of your maximum heart rate and gentle exercise relates to about 60% of your maximum heart rate.

Training Zone

To be effective in developing stamina it is best to ensure that the exercise session lasts for about thirty minutes within your heart rate zone. This will generally mean that you will spend about ten minutes warming up to your heart rate zone after your pre-exercise warm up, and about ten minutes cooling down again before your post-exercise cool down. Allow about one hour.

Remember, your heart rate takes time to drop and increase, so be careful. If you have any doubts about your physical condition, consult a doctor.

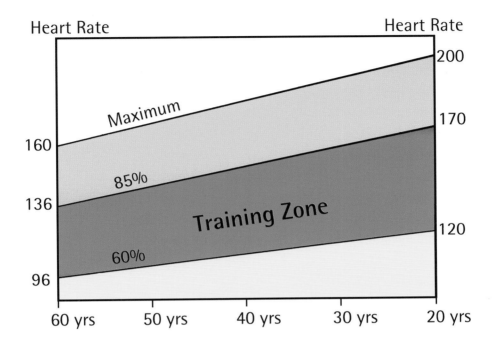

The training zone for endurance exercise

A Training Programme

To begin with, the level of training you require will depend on what you want to achieve and where you are at the moment. However, I have set out some guidelines below.

Freestyle is a very explosive sport, so too much endurance training can negatively affect your performance. It is probably a good idea to allow three days a week with a day's rest in between, for your endurance training. On these sessions develop those muscles that need to work in competitions, that is your upper body. If you wish to develop your overall endurance at other times you would probably benefit from using your legs more, for example cycling or running.

It is possible to vary the exercises in the three sessions you have chosen. Sometimes you may wish to swim, others you may wish to paddle, it may even be that the amount of daylight dictates your training needs. It is also useful to vary the routines to ensure good all round development.

One way of starting this routine would be to block three days in your diary and plan the sessions to be held on these days.

Day One

Day one, flat water paddling in a freestyle boat, could be something like this:

Warm up	15 minutes
Slow build up to medium speed	5 minutes
Maintain medium speed	5 minutes
Sprint	2 minutes
Maintain medium speed	4 minutes
Sprint	3 minutes
Maintain medium speed	3 minutes
Sprint	4 minutes
Maintain medium speed	2 minutes
Sprint	3 minutes
Maintain medium speed	3 minutes
Sprint	2 minutes
Slow decrease in speed	8 minutes
Cool down	15 minutes

Day Two

Day two could be a more steady style whereby fifteen minutes warm up is followed by thirty minutes medium speed paddling and then by fifteen minutes cool down.

Day Three

Day three may include the same level of warm up and cool down but set up so that the thirty minutes in between are a series of sprints with a very slow period in between. Each sprint could be over a set distance but getting faster or for a set time but covering more distance.

Summary

Developing your stamina will help ensure that you are able to paddle at your best when it counts. Increased stamina will also help decrease the tendency to develop injuries. There are a variety of ways to train for endurance and the most appropriate way will depend on your individual needs.

9.3 Suppleness

Suppleness has many benefits for canoe sport, not least of which is the fact that a greater range of movement in the muscles and joints of the body reduces the possibility of injury. Other benefits include the ability to maintain good posture whilst carrying out some of those more dynamic moves.

Stretching can be done for maintenance or developmental purposes. The same position is used in both types, however, the developmental stretch involves gently pushing the stretch a little further and holding the stretch for a few seconds more.

One way of developing suppleness is through the static stretch. Static stretches involve sustained, relaxed elongation of the muscle to be stretched (it does not involve bouncing or forcing to the pain barrier). It is best to focus on the muscle being stretched to ensure total concentration.

Basic Stretching

The basic stretch is used to ensure that your body is prepared to perform through its full normal range of movement. It should be carried out with care and slowly. The stretch position should be held at a point where gentle tension can be felt; if excess tension is felt then reduce the tension slightly. Relax mind and body as the position is sustained.

It is probably best to hold each stretch for about fifteen seconds and remember to breathe as you do. It is not a good thing to hold your breath whilst you stretch, you should be relaxed enough to not feel the need to do so.

The time to use this type of stretch would be in the warm up and cool down part of your training and competition routines. The routine that you develop can also be used to enhance your psychological preparation.

The Developmental Stretch

The developmental stretch carries the same care warnings as the basic stretch and should also be undertaken slowly. The main difference is that this type of stretching will help you increase your flexibility. The best time to carry out this type of stretching is when you are fully awake and very warm, ideally in a gym or bedroom or some place similar.

The stretch is held as the basic stretch, then, when the muscle starts to relax, you gently move further into the stretch until you feel the muscle lengthen again. This can be repeated a couple of times. Just make sure you are not feeling any pain and that your technique is accurate.

The Stretches

Sitting Groin Stretch

Works on the groin area.

This stretch is best carried out whilst sitting on the floor. Bend your legs and put the soles of your feet together a comfortable distance from your groin. Hold your feet and gently relax your body forward from the hips. Keep looking forward whilst stretching. Be careful not to arch the back.

Sitting Hamstring Stretch

Develops the back of the legs.

Sit on the floor with your legs straight out in front. Bend one so that the sole of this foot touches the inner thigh of the other leg. Ensure that the toes on the straightened leg point directly to the ceiling. Take hold of the straightened leg around the ankle and gently relax forward keeping the back straight and facing forward. Repeat again for the other leg. If you cannot reach your ankle, then put a towel around the foot and hold each end.

Lying Full Body Stretch

Stretches the whole of the body.

Lie on your back on the floor with your arms above your head. Stretch your whole body by reaching as far as you can with your toes and hands.

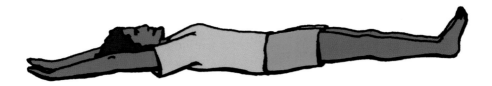

Seated Shoulder Stretch

Stretches the back and hip area.

Lie on your back with one leg bent. Take hold of this leg with the opposite arm and gently pull the leg across the body. Remember to keep the back of your shoulders on the floor. Repeat for other side.

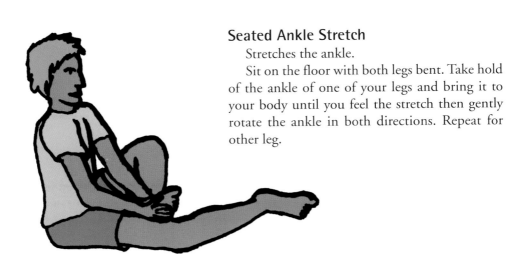

Seated Ankle Stretch

Stretches the ankle.

Sit on the floor with both legs bent. Take hold of the ankle of one of your legs and bring it to your body until you feel the stretch then gently rotate the ankle in both directions. Repeat for other leg.

Seated Thigh Stretch

Stretches the front thigh.

Sit with one leg bent so that the ankle is placed beside your hips. Make sure the top of the ankle is against the floor. The other leg should be bent, such that the sole of the foot touches the inner part of the first leg. Gently relax back until the stretch is felt.

Take care of your knees with this one, do not strain them.

Seated Shoulder Stretch

Stretches the shoulder and tricep.

Whilst sitting, take one arm across the front of the chest such that the hand rests on the opposite shoulder. Gently grasp the back of the elbow with the free hand and pull the arm across the body.

Seated Upper Back Stretch

Stretches shoulders, back and forearms.

Interlace your hands and straighten your arms out in front, at about shoulder height with your palms facing outwards. Gently extend the arms forward until the stretch is felt.

Seated Twist Stretch

Stretch felt in buttocks, side and lower back.

Sit with your legs out in front and bend one so that it crosses over the straight leg. Place the opposite elbow on the outside of the bent knee, whilst keeping your body supported with one hand behind you and your body twisted towards the bent leg.

Upper Body Stretch

Stretches the chest area.

Take hold of a towel at slightly wider than shoulder width and take the arms over the head whilst keeping them straight. Start with palms facing down.

Summary

You can use the same stretch routine in your warm up and cool down as you would use to develop your flexibility. The main difference is that the developmental stretches should only be carried out when you are very warm, preferably indoors, and that they entail a little extra persuasion on your part.

9.4 Diet

The fuel source of an athlete is the food and drink he or she consumes. As such what we eat and drink has a profound effect on our performance.

As with the other sections this is not designed to be the ultimate section on nutrition, more a pointer towards providing you with a guide to eating and drinking effectively.

In a nutshell, our bodies require different food and fluid substances for survival and optimum performance. These can be described as fats, carbohydrates, proteins, vitamins, minerals and water.

Fats

Fats can be found in plants and animals and are simply categorised as saturated or unsaturated. The experts tend to say that the unsaturated fats are the best to consume. Fats do play an essential part in the maintenance of our bodies. For example fats serve to protect major organs and act as an insulator against the cold. Therefore in an appropriate amount they are essential for the body's efficient functioning.

As a food substance, too much fat will be stored as emergency food. When you consider that the energy within a pound of fat is probably twice that within a pound of carbohydrates, you can see that it is easy to eat too much fat.

Saturated fats tend to be found in cakes, chocolate, red meat, chicken and dairy products. Unsaturated fats are found in peanuts, olive oil, fish and avocados.

Carbohydrates

Carbohydrates are also categorised in different ways, they are termed simple or complex carbohydrates. Simple carbohydrates are those found in fruits, and complex carbohydrates are those found in vegetables, potatoes and rice.

Carbohydrates are the easiest food substance for the body to turn into useable energy and therefore the most efficient food stuff for an athlete to make use of. The carbohydrates will be stored as glycogen in the muscles and liver, and used as a direct source of energy.

Proteins

Protein is a complex structure, made up of simpler structures called amino acids. The body needs a set number of different types of these amino acids before it can effectively use the protein.

Protein is found in both plants and animals, though not always in a form that includes all the required amino acids. In some cases it is therefore very important to mix food stuffs in order to ensure you ingest the right mix of amino acids. The role of proteins in our bodies is to aid in the building and replacement of tissues.

The food stuffs that contain all the amino acids required by the body are, in the main, meat, fowl, eggs, fish and dairy products. However, the percentage of protein within each of these foods will vary as, for example, red meat also contains a great deal of fat. Plants such as soya beans, rice, pulses and beans also contain elements of protein but need to be mixed effectively to ensure the body ingests the right mix of amino acids.

Vitamins and Minerals

Vitamins and minerals are essentially triggers that ensure that many of the body's essential functions, affecting such areas as our growth and metabolism, are carried out. Vitamins include substances such as Vitamin A, B (in its many forms), C, D, E, Niacin and so on.

The best way to ensure that a correct balance of the necessary vitamins and minerals is absorbed by the body is to eat a balanced diet of natural foods. The foods that are as close to their original state as possible will provide the best source of vitamins and minerals. Processed foods invariably lack the correct balance of nutrients. It is possible to supplement your intake of vitamins and minerals but this should not be necessary if your diet is sufficient.

Water

Water is probably one of the most overlooked nutritional essentials in paddling circles. We are sitting on the stuff! It is worth noting that if the body is lacking in fluids, fatigue and performance deterioration can quickly follow. Furthermore it does not take a great deal of fluid loss to create performance deterioration.

In Practice

The bad news with all this is that the staple diet of burger and chips is out. There is a small amount of nutritional value in this but not enough. It is rather like putting petrol into a moon rocket, it will probably work but I doubt it will get to the moon. The good news is that you will become far healthier all round and feel better in yourself if you start to adopt better eating habits.

For general nutritional purposes most of your food should be from carbohydrates. For effectiveness in freestyle you will probably want to consume about 50% of your daily intake as carbohydrates, about 30% as fats (of which the majority should be unsaturated), and the rest as proteins.

Supplements

The taking of supplements has always been a tricky point. In our sport there really is little need to take supplements, providing your diet is effective. Sometimes all that travelling

Performer's Top Tip - You 'arc' what you eat.

Just putting a little bit of thought into what you eat and drink leading up to a competition can make all the difference...

Personally, I am always aware of what I eat (good or bad) and when I am eating it. If I break one of my personal guidelines I will do an extra sprint the next time I am on the water to compensate, as a kind of punishment! I try never to eat late at night (say after eight o'clock), and leading up to a competition I'm especially careful.

When you start your 45 second run you want to feel fast and light... like nobody can catch you... you need to go like a rocket.

Don't over-eat the night before a competition and on the day eat light. My preference is cereal and bananas for breakfast and a can of Red Bull half an hour before I get on the water. Feel fast and light - it'll probably gain you a place or two in competition.

Shaun Baker is probably the world's best known extreme kayaker. He has been UK National Freestyle Champion some nine times and won over twenty major international competitions.

He is sponsored by Red Bull, No Limits Clothing, Sector Watches, SAS Institute, Teva Footwear, Dainese Safety Gear, Playboater, Eskimo, Werner, and Wild Water.

between venues does mean that you do not eat as well as you should do; in this case supplements that help ensure you consume the right balance of vitamins and minerals may well be of use.

Salt

Salt is an additive to many tinned and processed foods; we really do not need so much of it. If your diet is well balanced and contains a full quota of fresh vegetables and fruits you probably will not need to add any more.

Alcohol

Alcohol is a nutrient, though not a very effective one. Alcohol also has the added factor of wicked hangovers, when abused, which are definitely not conducive to optimum performance paddling.

Refined Sugar

Refined sugar (i.e. the stuff we put in tea or find in sweets and jam), has very little positive use if your diet is right. Refined sugars are used in many processed foodstuffs as a sweetener, yet there is minimal nutritional value in its consumption so it should take up no more than a small amount of your daily diet. The negative aspects to eating that chocolate bar are considerable. Firstly your body's natural mechanism for keeping blood sugar at an optimum level becomes disturbed. The role of insulin in the body is to ensure that the levels of sugar in your blood remains constant. When that chocolate bar is eaten blood sugar levels rise quickly, as a result an overdose of insulin is secreted to lower it. Consequently you feel an immediate rush of energy which is very quickly followed by weakness, hunger, dizziness, rapid heart rate and trembling. The normal response to this feeling is to eat another chocolate bar, however all you will be doing is starting off a roller coaster effect and destroying your body's ability to function effectively. Clearly it is far more effective to ensure that your body has enough energy by consuming more fruit and vegetables.

Summary

The food we eat has a vital part to play in how we perform, physically and mentally. Food also affects our health and well being, our body weight, our strength, and how well we get over injuries. Learning about nutrition is a vital part of achieving optimum performance and should not be taken lightly. You wouldn't expect a formula one car to function very well on inferior fuel, so why should you expect your body and mind to do it?

9.5 Conclusion

Training for physical fitness is hard work but the benefits will far outweigh the work you put in. You need to consider what level of fitness you currently have and which aspects need developing. Once this has been done and you are happy with the routine you wish to undertake, have fun with it.

Optimum physical fitness entails balancing the amount of strength you need, the amount of local and general stamina you need, and of course the fuel you use to provide the energy to carry out your training and competition routines. This chapter has outlined the basics required to ensure you give yourself the best chance, it is up to you to make the best use of the information and become the star that you know you can be.

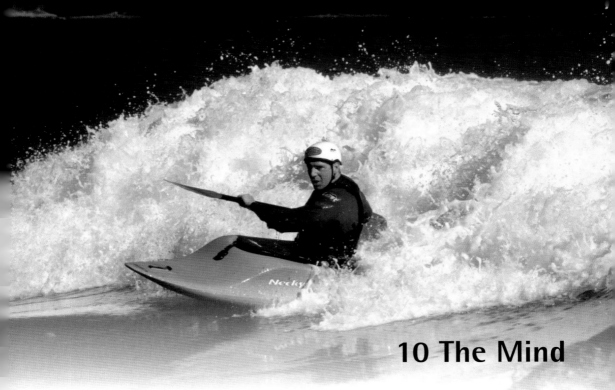

10 The Mind

Performing at a level that is consistent with your true potential requires mental training as well as physical training. Even the most technically skilled, tactically brilliant, and physically fit, will not perform to their optimum if they are not mentally proficient. If you concentrate on the wrong things, or cannot let go of mistakes or bad breaks, if your self-confidence is low, or you find handling the pressure of competition hard, you will need to develop your psychological skills. If you leave the mental side of performance to chance, then you are more vulnerable to performance problems like excessive nervousness, psyche-outs, choking, slumps and blocks. To be more consistently successful you have to learn to harness the power of your mind to help you think like a winner and develop mental toughness. This chapter considers some of the more usual situations, and how you can use some specific skills to help yourself.

First this chapter considers the development of peak flow and how important it is to ensure you connect with those feelings as often as possible. Then the use of imagery is investigated. Whilst imagery is useful for developing a number of other mental skills, it is also worth considering on its own merits. Imagery is a key factor in the effective preparation for competitions as well as in the development of self-confidence, the overcoming of fears, and the avoidance of psyche-outs and intimidation. Developing your skills in imagery will improve your practice sessions and increase your belief in yourself.

The third section considers stress management and how to handle over and under arousal. To perform at your best you need the ability to stay calm and composed under pressure. Choking and psyche-outs are often a direct result of ineffective stress management techniques. Learning how to understand yourself, developing the right techniques, and practising them, will help you stay cool and successfully manage your performance.

The fourth section discusses the importance of focus and how to develop winning concentration. Concentration is the key to performance excellence, and your focus before and during competition determines your ability to handle pressure and paddle at your true potential. Mental toughness is built around your concentration skills, so learning to focus on what is important and developing the skills to block out everything else is vital for consistent performance.

The fifth section considers the role of self-confidence. How you effectively deal with pre-competitive self-doubts and negative thinking will often make the difference between winning and losing. Learning to train your inner self so that you maintain appropriate levels of self-confidence will enhance your competitive edge. Equally the ability to bounce back immediately from setbacks, losses, and bad breaks is critical to your success.

The Coach's Perspective

As a coach, a working knowledge of mental skills training techniques will help you become more effective and therefore much more successful with your athletes. Knowing how to get the most out of others will help you avoid the mental traps that many coaches fall into. Learning mental skills will also enhance your technical skills, and give you the competitive advantage. Train your athletes to use mental toughness skills and they will regularly compete to their potential.

10.1 Peak Flow

The feeling of power and timelessness that occurs when you are physically and mentally inseparable from the activity you are undertaking is often termed flow. The purpose of mental preparation for competition is to ensure that you start your performance in this powerful, optimum state. Many high level athletes do this by developing routines that help them to focus their minds and block out distractions. These routines may involve complex and detailed dressing rituals, or precisely executed warm-up sequences that involve specific mental skills such as imagery and stress management. The end result is that competition runs are consistently performed at the highest level of skill and the performers feel totally in tune with themselves and their environment.

Achieving Flow

Flow is easiest to achieve when you consider that your skills are good enough to match the perceived difficulty of the competition and that the competition is not so easy that you become bored and do not concentrate. Flow will happen when you have distraction under control and you are paying full attention to the performance, with no analysis of errors or technique.

You will find that flow happens more when you are relaxed, alert and thinking positively. You have eliminated all negative thoughts. Flow cannot be forced, it should be allowed to develop. Flow will happen when you have trained effectively and are attending to the relevant cues.

Flow is when you are completely engrossed in an activity or performance to the exclusion of everything else. When you are in a state of flow, focusing intensely on the execution of skills, you will give your best performances. You enter a state of almost Zen-like meditation, in which dysfunctional moods, distractions and stressors simply have no place in your consciousness. You are free to execute skills just as you have trained yourself to execute them. Flow is an immensely satisfying state to achieve. Oriental martial arts, such as Karate or Kendo use this Zen approach in such concentration that the fighter is continually in a state of almost pure flow. The competitors seek to block out all distractions from their ego; they do not judge their performance, they are at one with their surroundings and they immerse themselves totally within the activity. Western sports psychology is now advocating an almost identical set of strategies through a skills based approach. You may appreciate a mystical approach; if so, then the Zen approach to focus is worth trying.

When all your attention is focused either on the skills or routine being performed, or on the input from your senses relevant to the sport, and you are fully focused on the activities being performed. When you are not aware of your own awareness, consciousness of self, or ego. When you are not evaluating the quality of execution of skills during performance, and not concerned with distractions such as results, judges, audiences or other people's expectations. When you are not making any conscious decisions in your mind, or reasoning with words. In that moment, you have achieved a state of flow.

In essence you are trusting your mind and body to follow their training and you are in complete control of actions and reactions. You will almost feel as if you are in an altered state of consciousness.

Adverse Effects to Achieving Flow

Many things can adversely affect the chances of achieving flow, for example, wanting to win or show off, or wanting to frighten or terrify your opponents. The chances of flow occurring can also be affected by being reactive and not taking the initiative, or trying so hard to achieve the correct state of mind that you end up being distracted.

The main purpose of the rest of the chapter about the mind is to provide a brief overview of some of the skills that will help you achieve this state of flow. However before we move on, there are a couple of things about the brain that would be worth considering.

The Physical Brain

Firstly your brain is extremely complex, and made up of a vast number of physical and psychological components. Much of its function is still not understood. One theory considers the brain to be separated into left and right hemispheres. The left performs analytical activities that are processed logically, and the right side of the brain is more holistic and intuitive.

The Hemispheres

The left or logical side of the brain (often called the Analyser), tends to be dominant in western society. It is believed that this part of the brain analyses and understands new skills, and examines existing techniques or attitudes for errors and faults. If this is so, the left brain would seem to be highly effective during training and when improving technique.

The right or intuitive side of the brain (also called the Integrator), controls the best performance of a skill by integrating all of its components into one flowing movement.

The Brain in Competition and Performance

These points are important in that either your analyser or your integrator should be dominant in different circumstances. An example of why this is important to understand can be seen when comparing training to competition. During much of training the analyser should be dominant, picking up errors and faults in technique, or harmful attitudes. It will then send corrections to the integrator to amend the complex skill. Letting the integrator control practice can end up in empty training, in which nothing new is learned. During performance, however, the Integrator should be in control, so that all the skills learned are performed in a completely coordinated, flowing way. The integrator is also more effective in making tactical decisions. Letting the analyser control performance by criticising or analysing execution of skills, distracts the integrator. You have achieved flow when your integrator is in complete control of a performance, and is not being distracted either by analysis from the left side of your brain, or by external factors. It is very important to appreciate that individuals will generally have a preference for either left or right brained thought, as such you should be realistic about your preference and develop the weaker side.

The Evolved Brain

The second consideration is that one of your brain's functions may be to protect you from danger. An important part of this is the response that draws your attention to unexpected or unusual stimuli. In the past this concept might have indicated that a predator was about to strike. Things that may stimulate this effect in freestyle competition are water conditions, loud noises (e.g. crowds or music), flashing lights (e.g. flash-guns), or movement (e.g. other performers). Another consideration is that anything that has not been experienced before can be distracting. In a natural environment, this drawing of attention is very important for survival. However, in a modern sporting environment these are distractions that break flow.

Summary

Part of learning to achieve flow is learning to isolate the important stimuli of the sport from the irrelevant ones that cause distraction. This will involve learning to selectively override your brain's natural reaction to stimuli. There are a number of ways to achieve a state of flow and some of the techniques that are relevant to freestyle are outlined in the following sections.

10.2 Imagery

Imagery (sometimes referred to as mental training and visualisation), is the use of the imagination to enhance your performance. The mind can be a very powerful aid to your training and competition performance if you learn to harness its power. Mind and body are linked such that if you think of an exciting rapid or something that scares you, your body will probably react to those thoughts. For example you may find your heart starting to pump fast or your muscles starting to twitch. Imagery is the process by which you can create, modify, or strengthen physical and mental processes by training purely within your mind. This section considers some ways to develop your imagery skills and some situations in which imagery may be useful.

Developing Imagery Skills

The key to using imagery is the ability to develop vivid mental pictures in a disciplined way. It is not about haphazard imagination, (though this is also powerful and a good place to start); it is about directing your mental processes in a structured way. One way of achieving real power in your mental rehearsal is to use all your senses in creating an image. Most people have the ability to feel (physically and emotionally), see, hear, smell and taste. Where possible, all these senses should be combined to develop a powerful image. When you create an image in your mind, make it as real as possible. Visually it may well be worth creating life-sized and sharp images that include precise detail, colours and movement. Physically you may find it useful to develop sensations such as the feeling of the paddle in your hand, the texture of your clothes, or the physical movement required for that specific technique, or even the feeling of flow when surfing. You may find it powerful to hear the roar of the wave or the swish of the blade as it slices through the water. The sweet smell of fresh air mixed with the pure taste of that mountain stream may transport you to your favourite wave. The feelings of excitement and power just before you start your run can be reproduced to strengthen your images. The trick is to develop all your senses to the best of your ability, so that you can use them to reproduce the experience in your mind. These sensations can be observed in real situations and then incorporated into imagery later, to develop more life like mental pictures.

A point to remember is that people have different strengths when developing images. For some, the physical sensations may be more powerful. If this is you, you may like to start your image development with physical movements. If you are very visual, consider creating a picture in your mind that is as vivid as possible before moving on to the next sense. It may also be that a specific situation, such as the smell of fresh bread, will automatically trigger one of your senses. If this is the case, go with the flow. The smell may trigger off a mental picture of soft succulent bread just out of the oven. This could develop into a sensation of taste when a piece of it is bitten off and the sweet strawberry flavour of the jam soaks into your mouth, followed by the sensation of the soft bread as it melts on your tongue. The physical action of buttering and biting may be next. As long as it works for you, use it but do not rest on your laurels. Imagery is a skill and does need working on to master. Your weakest points will need to become strengths if you wish to make the most of imagery.

To develop powerful imagery abilities you may need to start with something small. One way to do this is to hold a lemon in your hand and notice its texture, size, colour and shape. Smell and taste the lemon, and take note of how you are feeling whilst you are doing this. The next step is to evoke all these feelings when the lemon is not in your hand. Close your eyes and start recalling all those feelings, thoughts, tastes and smells whilst holding the imaginary lemon. It may be that the development of the skill takes some time to perfect, but then it probably took you a few years to develop your paddling skills; so be patient and keep practising.

When you are first starting to develop your imagery skills you will need to be relaxed and have a good idea of the real situation, so that you can recall all the details. Start by concentrating on the skills for a few minutes a day in a quiet place, then develop slowly so that you can use the skill in any situation. As you get better and start to use the skills in a freestyle context you may feel that checking your images against a video replay of the action or writing scripts for the intended images will help.

Internal Imagery

This type of imagery is where you are living the experience. In this instance you may be using your mind to develop an image of you surfing. In your mind you will be seeing the activity as if through your own eyes, you will be feeling the body movements and hearing the sound of the water as if you were actually on the water. Your body may be moving as you glide across the wave, your eyes may start to blink as you imagine the water splashing on your face. You may even feel the reactions of the boat as it dives or edges.

External Imagery

This type of imagery is where you watch yourself doing the activity. It may be that you create the same image of you surfing, but this time you decide to stand on the bank and watch yourself as you glide across the wave. You will be able to see your blades as they drive up the eddyline for that wave, or watch your body as it twists from right to left as your boat carves out that perfect pattern. You will be watching yourself as if on a video machine, though you may wish to add smells or other sensations to ensure a really vivid image.

Internal versus External

You may think that imagining yourself within your body, and feeling and sensing as if you were there would work more effectively as the image is more realistic, vivid and involved. However, research has shown that seeing images as if from a third party is also beneficial. It is probably most effective to develop your skills in internal and external imagery techniques.

Coach's Top Tip

Visualise a 'tube' running from the beginning to the end of your run. The tube follows the exact path of the run. Boat and body should stay within the tube. Therefore the tube will need to expand in either a lateral or vertical plane depending on the type of move.

As you become accustomed to the use of tubes, add colours depicting aggression levels required within the run. ie green = passive, blue = medium, red = aggressive.

Tubes can be a staggeringly effective tool, however it may go over your head if you are not skilled at visualisation. Be prepared to abandon it and come back to it later.

Jay Cooper is a freelance BCU level 5 Coach specializing in white water and play boating.

Imagery in Training

You can significantly improve the quality of your training sessions by using imagery effectively. You can focus on all the important parts of the skill by performing in your mind before you execute it. Imagining an activity before its execution helps you focus on the execution of skills, when otherwise you might just be tempted to go through the motions. It allows you to slow down and analyse fine skills or complex techniques to form as perfect a model of the technique as possible. It reminds you of what aspects to concentrate on for perfect execution of the skill. It allows you to assess how the physical movement compares with the perfect image, and helps you detect faults in your technique. Alternatively, if the technique was better than the image, the image can be adjusted.

In addition, imagery can be used in training to practice the other mental skills described in this chapter. Whether you are practising stress management skills or developing focus, imagery can be an important tool. You might use imagery to practice keeping good technique when your limbs feel exhausted, or to rehearse and perfect strategies that will be used during a real performance. You can use imagery to feel and practice moves and routines perfectly within your mind in order to prepare for events that cannot be easily simulated in practice. This will give you the confidence to deal with these events as they arise.

Imagery might be used for getting a feel for the experience of competition at a higher level. Imagery can be used to mentally practice when you cannot practice with mind and body, for example, when you do not want to tire yourself before a performance, or when you do not have the time or space to practice a particular skill in the more conventional physical way. If you ever get injured or equipment is not available, imagery may be useful.

Imagery in Goal Setting

You may even wish to use imagery to experience the achievement of a goal in your mind before you physically achieve it. This helps you to build the confidence that the goal can be achieved and expand your perceptions of the boundaries of your abilities. Practising with imagery helps you to slow down complex skills so that you can isolate and feel the correct component movements of the skills, and note where problems in technique lie.

Imagery is also useful as a tool for enhancing goal setting. By using the technique to visualise a recent performance you can gather feedback, and then use this feedback to adjust your goals.

Imagery in Competition Rehearsal

You may wish to use imagery as part of your warm up, or as a form of mental preparation while you are sitting in the eddy waiting for your turn. It may be that developing vivid images of yourself successfully completing your routine would help. You may decide that creating the feelings, thoughts and sounds that accompany success would greatly enhance your ability to perform in a smooth and flawless way. It may even be that you have practised a routine so well that all you need to do is recall the first (trigger) part of the sequence and the rest of the routine will follow. In this instance you could use imagery to ensure that you begin your routine in the right place on the wave.

Summary

Imagery is the disciplined use of the imagination to create clear and realistic images in your mind. Imagery can be used to practice physical skills when no other method of practice is available. It can be used to enhance your self-confidence and develop other mental skills. It can help you prepare for eventualities that are hard to simulate in reality, or aid in the development of focus before a skill is executed.

"An effective use of imagery will greatly enhance your performance."

10.3 Arousal Control

Being over stressed or anxious is often associated with spending too much energy focusing on, and trying to control those things that cannot be controlled. In freestyle this could mean concentrating on the judging, your opponents, the environmental conditions, or your admiring fans. It is also worth remembering that freestyle is only a part of life, so factors outside of competition, like exams or work can also effect your level of anxiety. If you focus on the factors that cannot be controlled, you will probably tighten up and 'choke'. It is also important to remember that you are responsible for your own stress levels. It is not the event itself that causes the feelings, but your beliefs about the event.

This section outlines some skills that will help you direct your focus and manage any competitive stress you may have.

Symptoms

The effects of being overstressed can be experienced physically, mentally, and behaviourally and the symptoms individually determined. It is also important to note that the symptoms could be caused by other factors. However, if you find yourself exhibiting a number of them, it would be worth investigating stress management techniques.

The Physical Symptoms are:
- Increase in heart rate
- Increase in sweating
- Cooler skin
- 'Butterflies' in your stomach
- Rapid breathing
- Tense muscles
- Dry mouth
- A desire to urinate

The Mental Symptoms are:

- Worry
- Confusion
- Inability to concentrate or difficulty in making decisions
- Feeling ill or odd
- Feeling out of control or overwhelmed

The Behavioural Symptoms are:

- Talking rapidly
- Nervous mannerisms like nail biting, foot tapping, increased blinking, twitching and pacing
- Scowling
- Yawning

Optimum Stress Levels

Each individual has an optimum level of arousal at which they perform best. It is just as problematic to be under aroused as it is to be over aroused. If you are under aroused your performance may suffer because you become bored and unmotivated. If this state persists for a long time, you may find the sport becoming tedious, and give it up. If you are over aroused your performance will suffer because you find it difficult to focus. Your flow can be disrupted, you can be distracted, and competition can become threatening and unpleasant.

In between these two levels is a zone of optimum performance. To give a high quality performance you will need to stay within this zone. Some people may operate most effectively at a level of stress that would leave other people either bored or over aroused. It is imperative that you take responsibility for controlling your own levels of arousal because individuals react differently. Someone who does badly in an unimportant competition may do well in an important competition and vice versa. You may also find that you need to be more relaxed whilst performing complex skills than for more basic skills.

Finding Your Optimum Stress Level

An effective way of finding the stress level at which you operate best is to record your subjective arousal symptoms in your training diary. Another way is to use monitoring equipment whereby you can get objective information for your diary. Review your diary periodically, to help you decide whether you need to implement a stress management programme. Stress management programmes are a combination of techniques that are used to manage your level of stress. In the main, they are designed to help reduce the level of arousal, however, techniques to increase arousal are also available.

Reduction of Arousal

Reduction of arousal will often be situation specific, sometimes to an extent that one wave on one river will trigger a state of anxiety, whilst if you were anywhere else you would not be concerned.

The Process

By concentrating on the importance of the competition, or your desire to win or avoid losing, or anything else linked to the end result of your performance, you will probably put excess stress on yourself. This type of focus distracts you from your performance and will often make you feel physically tight. The best remedy for this type of anxiety creation is to ensure that you focus on the process of achieving a win, not on the winning itself. Visualise the routine you will be using for your competition run and concentrate on being the best you can be.

Self Awareness

If you can develop an understanding of the relationship between your level of anxiety and how well you perform, you will have taken a major step towards handling pressure more effectively. If you can feel your anxiety before a performance, and are able to determine whether these feelings are good for performance or bad for performance, you will be better able to control them. You can then do something about your anxiety level before it is too late.

Coping Skills

Some off season training should be set aside for developing a number of mental skills that you can use to relax under pressure. The skills that work best for you will not necessarily work for others, so try a few before deciding which to use. These skills are generally called relaxation techniques. By having a couple of relaxation techniques in your skills repertoire, such as progressive muscle relaxation or deep breathing exercises, you will be better placed to choose the most appropriate. As you become more skilled at using these techniques you will find them easier to use.

Reframing

Reframing is a technique whereby you develop alternative responses to a stressful situation. For example, if you arrive at a competition where the weather is bad, rather than thinking negative thoughts like "I can't compete when it's cold," reframe them. Your new thoughts might be "everybody is going to feel down now because it is cold, so I'm going to warm up even more and make the best of what everyone else is feeling."

Reframing this type of adversity helps you use other adversities more positively. You will end up boosting your confidence rather than eroding it. An Australian rugby league coach once told me that if ever his team view a situation negatively he gets them to find three positive things about the same situation. By learning this process you will be able to develop ways to use adverse situations like poor weather conditions, bad scoring, or fatigue to enhance your performance rather than destroy it.

Humour

The surest way to get yourself to tighten up and paddle badly is by being too serious. Peak performance comes out of having fun. You do your very best when you are enjoying the competition. By using humour, you can help yourself stay loose, keep the game in perspective and perform like a champion. An athlete that is too serious is an athlete who has a tendency to choke under pressure.

Competition Importance

If you make the competition too important your performance will inevitably suffer. Try to keep a level head about the competition and your opponents. You may feel overstressed because of the potential for heavy financial awards or because family and friends are watching. Whatever the reason, if the event starts to take over, try to place the situation in a bigger context so as to minimise the effects.

Training

Specific training will help you handle the effects of over arousal. Training with competition in mind and including some of the pressures of competition will help. If you have trouble with certain aspects, like bad weather, then train in bad weather when possible.

Proactivity

When you forget about making mistakes you will find that you perform better. If you are worrying about messing up you will be distracted from the task in hand and find yourself tightening up and making the mistakes you were originally worried about. Let your mistakes go immediately and focus on what you want to have happen, not what you are afraid will happen. If you learn from mistakes and use them for feedback on how to improve, mistakes can be a very powerful force for change.

Self Identity

It is a mistake to equate yourself with your performance. By that I mean that just because you did not do so well in a competition it does not follow that you are a bad paddler or that you are a bad person. If you do not make this separation your performance will suffer. If

Lighten up! - Jon 'Pies' Smith (left) and Jim Shrimpton - Photo: Bob Timms

your ego is on the line every time you compete, you have a lot to lose. When you compete with a lot to lose, you will most likely get stressed out and paddle poorly.

Accept the Challenge

Focusing on the 'what ifs' of losing is the last thing you want to do before and during an important competition. It is better to challenge yourself and think that you can do it and to believe in yourself. You will more than likely rise to your challenges and respond poorly or inconsistently to any threats you may have made to yourself.

Focus

Focus on the aspects of your paddling that you have to do to compete well. Teach yourself to only look at, or listen to, things that keep you composed and performing at your best. Concentrating on the unimportant things like the crowd or other competitors will distract you.

Coach's Top Tip - Calm in the Storm

Try to focus on gaining areas of quiet during your performance, enabling you to review your plan and gather your thoughts as to where and what to do next within your routine. These calm areas can be both physical, as in a sweet spot on a wave or a point of stability on the top of the pile, or mental. Achieving mental calm takes practice, as often you may have a lot of external stimulus to deal with like, "Am I ever going to get out of this hole in one piece?" Using a wave or hole that you are comfortable in, develop the ability to think of other things. This can be anything from paddle tricks to abstract thoughts. As long as it is diverting your mind from the job in hand you will find that the side surf, for example, becomes automatic, thus allowing you to concentrate on setting up for the next element in your routine. As you become adept at being able to focus your mind you will find that you will be able to manage more and more complex routines as you develop calm spots in the storm to review and plan.

Dave Luke is a freelance BCU level 5 Coach specializing in white water and play boating in kayak and OC1.

Other Possibilities

Self-Hypnosis

Hypnosis is one of those 'mystical' concepts that has been much misunderstood. In essence it is a powerful process that helps an individual develop a state of mind in which they are very relaxed. Self-hypnosis is where you help yourself reach this state of relaxation and directly influence your own unconscious with affirmations and suggestions. You can use this process as an effective method to reduce stress and induce relaxation.

When you are learning the techniques you will need to find a quiet place where you will not be disturbed. When you become proficient you will be able to use the skill anywhere.

Before starting the process you should think about what you want to achieve. Sometimes self-hypnosis can be used to embed simple verbal affirmations that undo the damage done by negative thinking. Sometimes self-hypnosis can be used to imagine positive outcomes to stressful events. Whatever you choose it will be best to develop the wording or visual routine before relaxing yourself.

To initiate the process you may like to lie down, however sitting in a comfortable position will be fine. Once you have found your comfortable, quiet place you will need to relax yourself. One way of doing this is to close your eyes and imagine yourself on a warm, tropical beach. Feel the rays of the sun soaking into your muscles and gradually relaxing each one. As the sun soaks your body you will be able to hear the gentle 'whoosh' of the waves as they roll in and out; all the while the tension in your body is reducing. The motion of the waves may be in tune with your breathing, so that every time you breathe out your body lets go of more tension. You may like to say 'reeelaaaxxx' to yourself as you breathe out. As you continue, your shoulders will begin to relax and your body will begin to feel warm and comfortable, eventually your whole body will feel relaxed.

There are of course many ways to initiate relaxation (see below for examples), and you may already have your own favourite techniques. Some people like to imagine waves of relaxation running down their body from head to toes, washing out tension as they go. Others find that concentrating on their breathing and releasing tension as they breathe deeply in and out works well. You can use whatever technique you find the most effective in helping you relax completely. As you get more proficient you may well find that this process will only take a few seconds, however, in the beginning don't be surprised if the process takes some time and thoughts keep filling your head... that's normal.

Once you are relaxed you will need to deepen the effect. Again there are many ways to help you do this. Sometimes a simple set of suggestions like "I am feeling really relaxed" will be enough. However, to begin with you may require a little more help. One way of deepening the effect is to imagine that you are standing at the top of a set of ten stairs. As you look down you can see your slippered feet standing on a deep soft carpet. On either side of the stairs is a handrail that you can use if you wish. Gradually you take each step counting down the steps as you go. When you reach the bottom, imagine walking through a door in front of you and into a large dark room. A white screen covers the far wall and there is a comfortable chair in front of the screen. You can then imagine sitting in the chair and watching the screen. When you have finished the whole process, you can walk back through the door and up the stairs (counting back to one as you go), ready to take on the world. This is only one technique, there are many more.

By now you should be completely relaxed, so it is time to focus on your own suggestions. You may like to see yourself complete the stressful event positively on the screen or read the statements you have prepared as they pass before your eyes on the screen. Some people even try different options by running films of possibilities on the screen, so that they can choose the most appropriate. It may also be useful to add a trigger word or action in the process, so that whenever you need it, all you have to do is repeat it to recall the complete state of relaxation. It is also possible to combine all the above techniques, e.g. reframing, whilst in a deep state of relaxation.

Progressive Muscular Relaxation (PMR)

Progressive Muscular Relaxation is a physical technique for relaxing your body. Put simply, you tense up a group of muscles so that they are as tightly contracted as possible. Then, after a few seconds, you let go of the tension so that they are relaxed. Finally you consciously relax them even further. This method can be applied to one muscle group or all muscle groups depending on whether you want to relax just a single area or your whole body. One way of starting a whole body process is to begin with your feet and gradually work your way up your body, tensing and relaxing as you go. This technique can be combined with deep breathing or imagery, as in the self-hypnosis section above.

Imagery

Imagery can be combined with other techniques or used on its own. To be effective you should use your imagination to recreate a place or scene that you find very relaxing. It is often a good idea to use all your senses; imagine those relaxing sounds, feel the warmth of the sun, and develop an image that is full of colour and texture. The more intensely you use your imagination to recreate the place or situation, the stronger and more realistic the experience will be.

You can also imagine locking the stressful event in a large secure box. The box can hold the stress until you are ready to deal with the situation, after your event. Another useful technique is to imagine the tension flowing out of your body, through your feet and into the floor.

Deep Breathing

The deep breathing technique, mentioned under the self-hypnosis paragraph, can also be used on its own. First you should focus on a spot just behind the belly button, then breathe through your nose for a count of four seconds. Whilst breathing in, you should be aware of

Coach's Top Tip – The Vibe (Dancing)

Try paddling in time to and in the style of certain types of music .

Why? It's a good way of coaching the changing speed and aggression levels needed during a run. I use reggae with its strong mellow rhythms for calm, rave for a fast aggressive style and classical music for its changes of tempo. Music that changes tempo can be used to adapt parts of a run that need to be faster or slower.

How about having music playing on the bank? Funky! Or music being played through headphones (waterproof of course).

Jay Cooper is a freelance BCU level 5 Coach specializing in white water and play boating.

your stomach and chest expanding. Hold your breath for about two seconds then slowly force the air in your lungs out through your mouth for a count of four to eight seconds. During the breathing out stage you should focus on ensuring that your lungs empty. You may find it useful to count your breaths as they draw in air and develop an image of the air leaving your body as you release the air from your lungs. The most important consideration is that you should be totally focused on your breathing. To begin with, you will probably find it difficult to stop thoughts distracting you; be patient, it will come.

Whatever Works for You

Some people find listening to relaxing music or stress reduction tapes very useful. Others find concentrating on past successful or positive events very useful. The trick is to have a few of these skills in your tool-box so that you can use them at an appropriate time.

Increasing Stress Levels – (Psyching Up)

There may be times when you need to raise your level of arousal in order to perform effectively. When you are feeling bored, tired, or unmotivated because there is no serious competition, you may need to 'psyche' yourself up. As freestyle events take place in hazardous environments we can't afford to enter an event feeling unmotivated. However, this should not be confused with needing to feel angry.

If you do feel the need to psyche up, try warming up faster and harder, or imagining that you are in some serious water and need to feel powerful to survive. Music can work very well if the right type is used, as can reframing (see above) and self-talk.

Summary

Feeling that you are under or over stressed is not uncommon and there are many techniques to help you find your optimal state. You will need to be skilled in a few techniques so that you have some ready when you need them, especially if the feelings come about unexpectedly.

Remember you have no control over other people, they will not always do what you want. People have their own agendas and do what they want to do. They can have bad days and make mistakes as well.

It is not possible to be always competent because you only achieve competence at a new level by making mistakes. Further negative events can be caused by your own negative attitudes, and such attitudes can cause you to view neutral events negatively. Another athlete might find something positive in something you view as a problem. You can often change the future and even improve it if you train effectively, or look at things in a different way.

You need mental energy to be able to concentrate your attention and maintain good mental attitudes. Mental energy is often wasted on worry, stress, fretting over distractions, and negative thinking. Over a long competition these not only damage enjoyment, but also drain energy so that performance suffers. Making good use of your mental attributes, resting effectively between events and ensuring that you sleep properly, will also enhance your ability to combat the negative aspects of stress and help you perform at your best.

10.4 Focus

Effective focus is the ability to concentrate on the relevant aspects of a specific task. It is knowing what is relevant in your current situation and how to direct your senses and thoughts towards the relevant parts, whilst shutting out what is irrelevant. An example of focus in action is when you are so engrossed in your activity that time flies by and nothing has distracted you. On those occasions when you are more concerned about your adoring fans than the competition in hand, you are probably not properly focused.

Your ability to focus appropriately will depend on your ability to direct your attention in the most effective way. Attention can be internal, whereby you may need to focus on your thoughts or feelings, or external, where you may be focusing on the river. Attention can also be focused on narrow or specific aspects of a situation, such as the sweet spot on a wave, or on a large or broad set of information, where the whole wave requires consideration. These four attentional styles combine so that you may have a broad/internal focus, a narrow/internal focus, a broad/external focus, or a narrow/external focus. At some stage in your training and competition you will need to concentrate on one or other of the four varieties. The ability to effectively switch between each at the right moment is essential. Focusing on the whole wave, when you should be focusing on that cartwheeling spot, will negatively affect your paddling, as will focusing on negative internal thoughts when you should be focusing on holding the boat on its edge.

	Broad	**Narrow**
Internal	This may be when you need to concentrate on how tense your whole body is before competing.	This may be when you focus on specific feedback from your hand or hip or even your self talk.
External	This may be when you need to survey the whole wave in order to determine where to make that flat spin.	This may be when you need to concentrate on the sweet spot whilst you are doing those cartwheels.

For the purposes of this section we will be concentrating on those factors that interfere with your attention and therefore affect your ability to focus on the task in hand and your ability to perform at your best.

Distractions

Distractions are those events that damage your performance because they interfere with your ability to focus. Distractions interfere with the effective application of appropriate attention and the performance of good technique. The end result is often excess stress and the dysfunctional redirection of your mental energy. There are a number of ways that distractions can occur; some are internal and some are external. You will probably have your own list of distracting factors and events, however, some of the more usual ones are listed below:

- Attention from people you do not know
- Life stresses such as work problems
- The desire to impress people who are important to you
- Difficulties at home
- Sponsors and media representatives who may expect great things from you
- Other competitors
- Interference with your usual routines
- Members of your team
- Significant others who wish to chat whilst you are trying to prepare
- Unexpected good or bad performances
- Frustration as a result of mistakes or poor judging decisions
- Badly timed or unjust criticisms

When you prepare fully for the events that disturb you they will cease to be sources of distraction and may even become sources of inspiration. Remember, your opponents will also have events that disturb them. By being better at managing your own distractions you will be one step ahead of them.

Increasing Focus

Developing techniques to appropriately direct focus will help you prepare for distractions that will occur during your training sessions, pre-competition preparation and competitions. Effective use of the techniques will help you alternate between attentional styles quickly and effectively. The end result will be that you start your run in a positive and focused frame of mind, and will be able to compete at your optimal level.

Making the List

Your training diary will be a useful tool for developing a plan for combating those distractions. To begin with, make a note in the back of the diary of all the relevant events that take place before you compete (or train). Then list all the mental activity that you go through leading up to your run. As you get used to using a training diary this list will grow so it is probably a good idea to leave enough space to allow for this.

The next stage is to make a list of every distraction associated with the above events that might occur. Then note down your solutions to the distraction and what you will do if your first solution does not work.

The fact that you have prepared for the potential of distractions will help, as the distraction will no longer be a surprise. However the solution is not always that easy so making lists of 'what to do if...' will ensure that you have prepared for almost all of the obvious eventualities. You will also feel more in control as you have developed strategies to deal with any distraction that may come along. Once you have made the list, it is worth attaching a positive trigger word to the new actions so that if the problem occurs you only need to think of the trigger word to start the sequence of solutions. Remember, it is not the event itself that causes the distraction, it is your belief about that event.

Positive Thinking

The ability to think positively and treat petty irritations as just that, is one way of counteracting distractions. Recognise that it is a petty distraction and let it go. This is often more difficult that it sounds. If this is the case, write down the problem and its effect. Then consider what your belief about the problem is. For example, the problem may be that photographers are very close to the wave when you are competing, and the effect may be that your performance suffers. Write these two points down and define the belief that actually causes the poor performance. In this instance it may be your belief that the photographers will be in your way that affects your performance.

The trick is to gather evidence that disputes your belief. This may be that others have not been affected, or that you will be too busy doing well to even notice them. Through the gathering of evidence that disputes your belief about the situation, and positive thinking, you will be able to help yourself stay focused.

Understanding Freestyle

Understanding the different aspects of freestyle and how to direct your attention will be a great help. Different waves and different techniques will require a different style of attention. Sometimes you will need to be focused on the whole wave. At other times you will need to be focused on the specific cues that your body gives. When you are reverse surfing it is very difficult to see what is happening, so more emphasis should be placed on attending to your body or the reactions of the boat.

It is worth spending time studying the wave before the competition so that you are able to work out what is going to happen where. This way you will already start preparing for any potential eventualities. By understanding the cues to look for, you can separate out the things to which attention should be directed from the clutter of irrelevant stimuli that occur in a competition environment.

Training

Like any other skill you can improve your ability to switch attention. One way of doing this is to study an object for some time so that you become engrossed in what it looks like and sounds like, what colour it is, what shape it is, what smells it has, what it feels like. Then switch attention to a different object and do the same thing. Eventually you will be able to switch focus very quickly.

This exercise can also be used to develop just one of your senses, thus if you are always distracted by sounds or thoughts then try the exercise by concentrating on sounds only or thoughts only. Whilst this exercise can be completed at home, you will need to take your new found skills on to the wave and work on it so that you have the skill perfected by the time the competition starts.

Imagery

An in-depth look at imagery is covered elsewhere. However, in this instance, you can visualise yourself performing a skill whilst focusing on its execution as you actually perform it. Feel the flow of the skill as it unravels in your mind; don't judge yourself or the skill, just let it happen.

Goal Setting

You may find that the longer you compete in freestyle the more likely you are to lose focus. There are a couple of reasons for this. It may be that as your reactions become automatic they hold your attention less, or that because you are more skilful you do not feel suitably challenged by other competitors. These focus problems can often be overcome by effective goal setting. Remember that goals are best set so that you are concentrating on the process and not the end result. Thus if you set appropriately challenging goals that ensure you keep developing your own skills, you will be enhancing your ability to focus.

Emotional Control

You may find that your mood on the day can adversely effect your ability to focus. Dysfunctional moods such as bad temper, unhappiness, lethargy and sluggishness, may make you more prone to negative thinking. This is distracting in itself and can often trigger bad moods in other people, which of course bounce back to you. You are in control of your moods despite how you may feel at the time. Allowing your moods to take over will not help you perform to your undoubted ability. Reframe these moods by visualising really positive scenes, or recalling more functional moods. It is also useful to concentrate on your goals and break them down into very small chunks that are separated from each other but in sequence. That way if one very small chunk is messed up you can immediately move on to the next. One of the most useful techniques is to force a smile, quite often the smile will take over and your mood will lift.

Summary

Coping with distractions and minor irritations is mainly a matter of attitude. You have a choice, you can either dwell on them and blow them up out of all proportion, or you can accept them and bypass them. If you waste mental energy fretting over a trivial problem, then it cannot be spent maintaining good technique. Over long events or competitions, this wastage of mental energy can seriously damage your performance.

It is worth remembering that when you are distracted, lose concentration and make a mistake, you have not lost your skills. All you have lost is your focus.

10.5 Confidence

Self-confidence is arguably one of the most important mental attributes that you will develop. It is a reflection of your feelings of self-worth, and can play an important part in determining your happiness throughout your life and your sport. In fact the difference between high and low self-confidence in sport has been linked to the difference between high and low success in competitions. Overconfidence will also have detrimental effects on your freestyle performance.

Freestyle can be both enormously effective in improving self-worth, and highly destructive in damaging it. When freestyle is performed with creativity and enjoyment, the chances for increased self-worth, and therefore self-confidence, are high. When your ego is on the line and the pressure builds up, the chances for damage to your self-confidence increase.

You may find that you have an optimum level of confidence that enables you to perform at your best. You will probably find that if you are functioning at your optimal level, mistakes will be learned from; they will not cause shock or a lowering of your levels of self-confidence.

Low Self-Confidence

Low self-confidence is when you feel that you do not possess the skills or talent to be successful in your task. If this type of feeling grabs you, a tiny mistake can seem enormous and could badly effect you. The little mistake could go on to reinforce your negative feelings and make you feel even worse. This in turn triggers off a self-fulfilling prophecy, and you end up competing just as badly as you thought you would. The spiral continues twisting its way down and this low self-confidence develops into a poorer performance, which in turn increases the feelings of self-doubt and low self-confidence. Feelings of low self-confidence may develop from a fear of failing, a lack of concentration, or negative thoughts. You may find yourself accepting blame for mistakes that are not your fault. These thoughts will inevitably fill your mind and disrupt your flow.

Overconfidence

In freestyle, overconfidence can be very dangerous, especially if it leads you into severe situations that you do not have the ability to get out of. In less serious situations, such as competitions, overconfidence can set the scene for a serious failure. The failure may well develop into feelings of low self-confidence, especially as your ego may well be battered because of the failure. Overconfidence is often based on an unrealistic assessment of your own ability. Sometimes these assessments may be as a result of misleading information provided by family members or well meaning friends who are trying to help you without taking your abilities into account. Sometimes the cause may be your own vanity or ego.

Techniques for Building Self-Confidence

There are many techniques to help you build the level of self-confidence that you need to perform at your best. Three of these techniques are Goal Setting, Mental Rehearsal and Positive Affirmations. Self-hypnosis is also a very useful strategy and is reviewed under the section on stress.

Goal Setting

One way of building appropriate levels of self-confidence is through proper use of the goal setting skills we mentioned earlier. In fact goal setting is probably the most effective way of building self-confidence. By setting measurable goals, achieving them and setting new goals, you prove your ability to yourself. You will be able to recognise and enjoy your achievement, and feel real self-worth.

It is important to know what you are capable of achieving, so that you do not end up failing. It is often a good idea to ask your training partner or friend to help you make a reasonably accurate assessment of what your true abilities really are. That way the assessment will have a greater chance of being free of ego or vanity. Effective goal setting and monitoring of achievement of goals can build self-confidence as targets are reached and improvement in performance is noted.

Imagery

Imagery in mental rehearsal is useful in building self-confidence when it is properly applied. Mental rehearsal, as used in confidence building, can be used as part of your practice routine or as part of your competition performance. In the former, you may choose to use your imagination to recall the feelings, sights and sounds of a successful cartwheel action or perhaps a whole routine (if you use a routine). Then once a day you can run the routine in your head and perfect it. Mental rehearsal could be used in a competition by adding the mental routine to your competition warm up or perhaps as part of your preparation just before your run.

You will remember from the section on imagery that images can be developed in two ways; either you can be part of the imagined activity or you can be watching it from the side. Ideally you would be best developing the ability to use both. The ability to develop these images is individually determined so comparing your images to the images of others is not always conducive to building confidence. For instance, I know of one athlete who is able to be part of the action but can only watch the action from the bank if the images are a series of black and white still photographs. This athlete is very successful.

Mental rehearsal could be used to imagine the achievement of a goal that is being worked towards in order to help you to believe that the goal is attainable. Remember that you need to have the ability to achieve the goal. If confidence boosting is required you may want to set the goals a little easier, then gradually increase goal difficulty to stretch yourself.

Mental rehearsal is a very useful tool to help develop emotional self-confidence and remove those factors interfering with your ability to achieve what you know you are rationally capable of. Overestimation of your true abilities can easily lead to overconfidence.

Positive Affirmations

Positive affirmations are simply positive statements. These may be in the form of positive self-talk or positive statements made by your coach or training partner. The technique is similar to reframing as described in the section on stress control. If negative thoughts enter your mind then use those pre-practiced positive phrases to reframe the thoughts. Some people yell words such as "STOP!" (out loud or in their head) to counteract negative thoughts. If this works then use it. Others prefer to use positive trigger words that focus on the behaviour you want to achieve rather than the behaviour you want stopped. Whichever way works for you, the trick is to use this trigger word to initiate the positive phrase and therefore the new functional action. These phrases need to be practiced as any other skill would be.

It is a good idea to develop your training diary so that you include your feelings of confidence, this way you will be able to assess if situations are similar and develop effective routines.

Summary

Self-confidence can inhibit or enhance your ability to take risks, and risk taking is an important aspect of developing your skills and competition performance. You need to have enough confidence in your own ability to handle any situation effectively. If you lack self-confidence then you will not take the risks that need to be taken. If you are over-confident you may not try hard enough and end up losing, or worse, you may try something that is way beyond your ability.

Self-confidence should be based on a realistic assessment of your true abilities. It can be developed through the achievement of well-formed goals. Self-confidence will be enhanced if your success is based on well practiced physical skills, a good knowledge of the sport, respect for your own competence, adequate preparation, and good physical condition.

10.6 Conclusion

Chaper 10 has covered a number of the most usual mental considerations in becoming the best freestyle paddler that you can be. First we considered the importance of performing in a state of flow, then we considered ways that you can develop your imagination to help maximise your freestyle abilities. We went on to consider ways to manage your own levels of stress, focus and confidence, so that you can increase your potential to consistently perform at your best. The bottom line is that it requires a commitment on your part to develop the necessary mental skills needed to be a world class performer. These skills will require as much of your time and energy as you use in learning and mastering the technical aspects of freestyle. The plus point is that once you have acquired the ability to be mentally at ease, and are consistently performing at peak flow, your performance will take on a new level of excellence. You will be a true master of freestyle, and be able to consistently perform at your very best.

11 Training Revisited

In the previous three chapters we have seen how planning your training sessions, and developing physical and mental fitness, can help you become the freestyle paddler that you know you can be. It is undoubtedly true that there is no quick fix solution and that you will need to work hard to realise your dream. The plus side is that if you really believe in your dream, and freestyle competition is part of that dream, the hard work will be worth it. You will need to be incredibly committed and develop a mastery of all the concepts covered in this part of the book, but if your dream is to be world champion and travel the world as a professional paddler, the commitment will be worthwhile.

You will need to be brutally honest about your level of ability and desire to improve. Whether you need to improve your imagery skills or your physical fitness, a degree of planning is essential, as is the ability to ask for help and guidance. You may find that a mentor or coach can help you pinpoint your weak areas so that you can develop them. Equally, having a training partner to hold the video camera whilst you train will be of considerable use.

Many of the skills highlighted in Part Three will also be of considerable benefit to the recreational freestyler. For that matter, you will find benefits in applying them to everyday life.

The Future of Freestyle

Predicting the future is the vocation of those who like to be proved wrong...

The last ten years have seen a period of amazing development in terms of both white water equipment design and of what is being done in that equipment; from non-retentive vertical moves to complex linked moves both in holes and on green waves, from groups of boaters getting together for laughs at rodeos to formal freestyle world championships and a structured judging system. This speed of development looks set to continue well into the new millennium as boaters push the limits of what can be achieved and manufacturers respond with increasingly specialised designs in order to make these limits achievable.

At the risk of being proved wrong, we will hazard a guess at probable developments within the sport, and look ahead to see what the future may hold as more and more boaters enter the strange world of the wave riders and hole shredders.

The early origins of freestyle kayaking began as boaters showed off their river running skills in craft used for creeking, rock bashing and surfing. One boat was generally sufficient for all aspects of the sport, although a few boaters were reported to have as many as two! As boats have become more freestyle specific, their usefulness for deviant river running has decreased and the term 'park and play' is an accepted phenomenon. Many boaters now have a quiver of kayaks from which to choose, depending on the water conditions and duration of the anticipated play session.

Enlightened boat manufacturers have responded to the demand for a single boat that can be used for all purposes by producing boats which generally fall under a new category; the river running playboat. Under this category fall such innovative designs as the Eskimo Quadro, Perception's Method and Method Air, and Pyranha's Inazone. Broadly speaking these boats share common features which allow considerable play potential, flat hulls and reasonably hard rails. They differ from freestyle specific designs in that they tend to have higher volume and a greater degree of comfort. This allows such boats to be used on longer river trips without undue distortion of the feet.

This recent burst of river running designs has happily coincided with a flurry of new moves which are not retentive and which would therefore be of little use to the competitive freestylist. Wave wheels, hammers and kick flips (a super modern move in which the boater flips the boat 360° on the horizontal axis while airborne off the back of a steep wave, an airborne barrel roll) are incredibly impressive and require considerable skill, but in a competitive environment would require a lung bursting, time consuming and point sapping slog back up the eddy.

Considering this we may pose the question: Is freestyle itself beginning to diversify? Will we soon see two related, but essentially different disciplines within the sport? One is freestyle as we know and love it now, shredding a single river feature or a very short section in order to achieve a structured point score, and a new aspect where the freestylist leaves the confines of the single wave or hole and takes on the entire rapid, combining retentive and non retentive, even aerial, moves as he or she descends? This would be similar to the difference between 'pro' board surfing and amateur surfing.

The increasing costs involved in having numerous state of the art boats introduces the possibility that competition will become dominated by a small core of professional boaters. In the manufacturers' quest for the design and marketing edge, the 'pros' would be given models that are fresh off the drawing board, leaving the amateurs to struggle in 'last year's model'. This would result in competition becoming increasingly distant from its roots and unattainable for non-sponsored paddlers, simply because they cannot afford to purchase the latest design. The 'catch 22' is that, should this happen, sponsors might lose interest in a competitive discipline that the majority of freestyle paddlers no longer identified with. Freestyle competition, if it is to remain healthy and vigorous, has to remain attainable and accessible to all, not just the preserve of a lucky few.

Perhaps the only certainty is that freestyle will remain, as it is now, essentially non-competitive. Most paddlers who consider themselves playboaters rarely, if ever, enter a freestyle competition and, although competitive boaters receive considerable recognition, there are undoubtedly many more out there who simply paddle for laughs with their friends. In essence these are the boaters who remain true to the sport's origins, the ones who playboat with the emphasis on play.

That's it, enough... we're off boating!

Acknowledgements

The publisher and authors of this book would like to extend their thanks to everyone who helped in the writing and production of this book.

In no particular order they are:

Bill Mattos, Pete Astles, James Shrimpton, Bleddyn Lloyd, Greer Mackenzie, Lisa Ferrero, Nuala Mulholland, Barney Caulfield, Shaun Baker, Jason Smith, Darryl Sergisson, Bob Timms, Franco's wife Joan (for putting up with Tom every Sunday evening), Jon 'Pies' Smith, Jonny Pearson, Allan Ellard, Deb Pinniger, Paul 'Cheesy' Robertson, Martin Tapley, Mark Birkbeck, Chris and Helen Gould, Paul Cripps, Paul 'Skinny' Jones, Lara Tipper, Ed Lock (Tom's landlord whose computer he took over), Tom Debruslais, Colin Hill, Dave Luke, Jay Cooper, Ray 'the rescue' Goodwin, Simon Westgarth, Tim Thomas, Dave Newport, Canolfan Tryweryn, Influence Whitewater Rafting, Drift Nepal, Dave Manby, KB Gurung, Craig Dearing, Danny Noblett, Nick Targett, Paul Targett, Andy 'Snakey' Whiting, Heather Gunn, Helen Metcalf and Paul O'Sullivan.

We would also like to thank Palm, Pyranha, Peak UK, and Nookie for the great photographs they made available.

I think that's it but there is bound to be more! Apologies if we left anyone out.

Glossary

Back loop	Movement where boat moves vertically end over end starting with the stern.
Boil line	High point of upstream foamy water below hole or stopper.
Bow	Front end of boat.
Bow draw	Draw stroke to move the bow of the boat.
Break in	Moving from an eddy into the current.
Carving	Putting the boat on edge with speed.
Catch	The moment the paddle pulls the water.
Charc	Term used by squirt boaters to describe the change of arc that takes place throughout a move. Also refers to approach and commitment.
Double pump	Two linked strokes used to 'oscillate' the boat.
Drive face	Part of the paddle that pushes the water, concave side of blade.
Eddy out	Moving from an eddy into the current.
Edging	Lifting one edge of the boat.
Face (wave)	Upstream-facing side of wave.
Feather	Angle of blades in relation to each other.
Ferry glide	Crossing the moving water using the current to assist, and angling the boat upstream so as not to lose ground.
Flat spin	Spinning the boat with no elevation.
Focus	Precise concentration on relevant and appropriate aspects of a situation or event.
Front loop	Movement where boat moves vertically end over end starting at the bow.
Goal setting	Organised definition and planning for a specific purpose.

Green water	'Solid' green part of wave.
High brace	Support stroke keeping the boat balanced, performed by pulling down on the drive face. Performed incorrectly it is a dangerous form of brace liable to separate shoulder from paddler.
High brace pull	Pull stroke done whilst boat is vertical on end, where pressure is exerted on the drive face of the paddle.
High cross	Crossing from one eddy to another using the upstream 'slope' of a wave.
Imagery	Disciplined use of the imagination to create the sounds, pictures, feelings etc. of a specific event or situation.
Initiate	Starting a move.
Inside edge	Edge of a boat on the inside of a turn.
Loose	Ability of the boat to slide and spin on the face of a wave.
Low brace	Support stroke, performed by pushing down on the reverse face of the blade.
Maw	Point at which wave and hole meet.
Moguls	Big lumps of snow.
Pile	Frothy bit of a hole.
Pocket	See maw.
Popout	Standing boat vertical on its end.
Power face	Same as drive face.
Power flip	Cute new capsize move (very fast) when you can't keep an edge up.
Power stroke	Normally the most vertical part of the forward paddle stroke.
Pre-rotation	Anticipating the movement of the boat by rotating your body.
Pry	Pushing stroke using non-drive face of paddle.
Purling	Bow of the boat plunging into green water.
Ramp	Sloping part of green water leading into rapid or wave.
Retain	Any movement that puts the boat back in its original position relative to a water feature.
Reverse face	Opposite face to the drive face of the blade, convex side of the blade.
Stern	Back end of boat.
Stern pry	Short and effective push stroke at the back of the boat using the paddle.
Stern push away	As stern pry but bigger and brasher.
Stern rudder	As stern pry but with less push, the paddle then resists the forward movement of the boat to 'steer'.
Side surfing	Sitting sideways in a hole.
Sweep stroke	A stroke used to turn the boat.
Tendinitis	Unfortunate and painful injury as a result of inflammation in the wrist area (in the case of kayakers).
Transferring edge	Moving boat from edge to edge.
Transition	Moving from one type of movement to another.
Trim	Balance of boat from front to back usually achieved by moving body weight.

Bibliography

Kayaking

Dutky, P. (1993). **The Bomb Proof Roll and Beyond,** Cordee, Leicester.

Ferrero, F. (1998). **White Water Safety and Rescue,** Pesda Press, Wales.

Neally, W. (1986). **Kayak,** Menasha Ridge Press, Birmingham, Alabama.

Whiting, K. (1998). **The Playboater's Handbook,** The Heliconia Press, Inc., Ontario.

Training

Addleman, F. G. (1984). **The Winning Edge: Nutrition for Athletic Fitness and Performance,** Prentice-Hall Press, NY.

Anderson, B. (1981). **Stretching,** Pelham.

Astrand, P. & Rodahl, K. (1986). **Textbook of Work Physiology,** 3rd Ed., McGraw-Hill, Singapore.

Butler, R. (1996). **Performance Profiling,** The National Coaching Foundation, Leeds.

Cabral, P. & Crisfield, P. Ed. (1996). **Psychology and Performance,** The National Coaching Foundation, Leeds.

Covey, S. R. (1989). **The 7 Habits of Highly Effective People,** Simon & Schuster, London.

Crawford, R. (1998). **How High Can You Bounce,** Vermilion, London.

Dilts, R. B. & Epstein, T. A. (1995). **Dynamic Learning,** Meta Publications, California.

Enomiya-Lasalle, H. M. (1987). **The Practice of ZEN Meditation,** Thorsons, London.

Goleman, D. (1997). **Emotional Intelligence,** Bantam Books, NY.

Hale, B. (1998). **Imagery Training,** The National Coaching Foundation, Leeds.

Hardy, L. Jones, G. & Gould, D. (1996). **Understanding Psychological Preparation for Sport,** John Wiley & Sons.

Linden, A. (1997). **Mindworks: NLP Tools for Building a Better Life,** Berkley Books, NY.

Reilly, T. Ed. (1981). **Sports Fitness and Sports Injuries,** Faber & Faber, London.

Rosser, M. (1995). **Body Fitness and Exercise: Basic Theory,** Hodder & Stoughton, London.

Seligman, M. E. P. (1998). **Learned Optimism,** Simon & Schuster, NY.

Schwarzeneger, A. (1985). **Encyclopedia of Modern Bodybuilding,** Penguin Group, London.

Sharkey, B. J. (1984). **Physiology of Fitness,** Human Kinetics Publishers, Inc., Illinois.

Sugarman, K. (1999). **Winning the Mental Way,** Step up Publishing, CA.

Thomas, V. (1975). **Exercise Physiology,** Granada Publishing Ltd., Hertfordshire.

Trower, P., Casey, A. & Dryden, W. (1988). **Cognitive Behavioural Counselling in Action,** Sage Publications, London.

Wann, D. L. (1996). **Sport Psychology,** Prentice Hall, NJ.

Zebroff, K. (1995). **Yoga for Everyone,** Foulsham & Co. Ltd., Berkshire.

find
the
sweet spot

www.**LENDAL**.com

Competition Scoring

In order to progress as a freestyle paddler you will probably want to enter a competition or two at some stage. Naturally it is a good idea to understand the rules of the game before you actually go for it. In this section, well-known British freestyle judge 'Hippy' Dave Newport clarifies the rules of the game as they stand at the time of going to press. As the sport progresses these rules are likely to change, and in international competition other judging criteria may apply.

'Hippy' Dave

Freestyle Competition

Freestyle is a dynamic and fast-growing area of paddlesport, with new moves constantly being created. As a result, developing a set of defined rules on which to score competition events has proven difficult. As yet there is no universal standard of rules, however many countries are now moving in the same direction. In the forefront of this movement is Britain, and it is the British judging scheme that this section is based on. At a British ranking event there are always at least three judges, one variety judge and two technical judges.

The technical judges award points purely on the basis of the position of the boat in or on the hole or wave, based on 180° direction changes and verticality. The variety judge awards points solely on the basis of the number of different moves completed by the paddler.

Technical Scoring

Changing the direction of the boat is the underpinning element on which technical points are awarded. To be recognised as a change of direction the boat must rotate 180°. This can be achieved by spinning the boat or elevating the boat as outlined below:

Spinning the boat 180° flat scores 1 point. Changing direction 180° elevated (at an angle of 45° or more) scores 2 points. Changing direction 180° vertical (at an angle of 70° to 110°) scores 3 points.

From the points system above we can work out a score for most moves, e.g. a 360° flat spin would score 2 points, as there is no elevation involved. However a cartwheel that consists of two vertical ends would score 6 points, and a cartwheel that consisted of one vertical end and one elevated end would have a lower score of 5 points.

The above moves all have an underpinning 180° change of direction and score. If however a competitor elevates their boat or takes it to the vertical plane, but fails to achieve a 180° direction change, this will be classed as a failed move and not scored. Additional points are awarded for the following moves:

Clean spin, 2 additional points per 180°.

Clean cartwheel, 2 additional points per elevated or vertical end.

Clean blunt, 3 additional points.

*Clean moves are recognised as a move being completed without the use of any paddle strokes. Ideally competitors should lift their paddles clear of the water when performing a clean move, this will show that they intended to perform a clean move and eliminate any confusion.

Split wheel, 2 additional points (one end must be elevated and the other vertical). The split must be completed when the boat is in the elevated or vertical plane. It is common for less experienced competitors to perform the split when the boat is not quite elevated thinking it has been scored. This can also catch out less experienced judges.

Loop, 6 additional points. Loops are recognised as the paddler starting from the upright position, pulling an end through the vertical plane, then pulling an inverted end back through the vertical plane so as to end up retaining the hole in the original position.

Crossbow initiations, 2 additional points per move (for elevated moves only).

Aerial moves: 2 additional points. An aerial move is any move completed when airborne. Moves only half completed in the air are not awarded the additional points.

Other scoring moves:

Front surf, 1 point.

Back surf, 2 points.

A surf is recognised as the boat being established on the wave or in the hole (facing upstream for front surf and downstream for a back surf) without the need of power strokes to hold position, rudder strokes are accepted. The surf must be maintained for at least two seconds or two cutbacks. Side surfing is not recognised.

Using all the information above, and by breaking down the competitors moves into their finer points such as split wheels, clean ends and spins, the technical judges can accurately score a run. The judges need to be competent enough to score the moves as they happen. However, the moves can come and go at a very fast rate and therefore two technical judges are required to give a score. A mean average is then taken from these scores and this is what is awarded for the run.

Variety Scoring

Variety scoring is a good way of encouraging the competitor to show a good range of moves as the variety score has a major influence on the overall result. The variety judge is purely looking out for the amount of different official moves* completed by the competitor.

The variety score starts at 1 point and the score increases by 0.25 points for every different move completed. The variety judge will only score a move once per run, so lots of different moves make the score bigger.

*The BCU Freestyle Committee publishes a list of official moves every year, below is the current list:

flat spin 360°, pirouette with a rotation of at least 180° in the vertical plane, cartwheel with a minimum of two ends, clean cartwheel one stroke permitted per two ends, split-wheel, loop, blunt, reverse blunt.

Moves that can be performed on either hand such as cartwheels are counted separately, so a right hand cartwheel is counted as a move and a left hand cartwheel is counted as a different move. If they both appeared in the same run the variety judge would award two sets of 0.25 points. This also applies to flat spins and splitwheels.

Overall Scoring

Once the mean average technical score is attained it is multiplied by the variety score giving the overall score for the competitor's run. At most events the competitors have two runs and these scores are added together to give their overall event score.

Timings and Boundaries

To run a competitive event fairly there needs to be set timings, boundaries (areas in which the competitors are judged) and water conditions, as well as the scoring format.

Timings

The timings for most events in the UK are two runs of 45 seconds duration each. This may seem like quite a short time, but it is common for competitors to tire quickly at this level of competition. It is therefore far better to give them two short runs with a small respite in-between. If the rest is too long it will allow the competitor to cool off, so organising the competitors to run in groups of about ten gives a good balance between performance and rest.

Timekeeping is very important, so it is advisable to appoint a responsible and reliable person whose only job is to timekeep. The competitors should be called for their run by an allocated judge who will be responsible for making sure that the judging panel are aware that the run is about to start. The timer should be started as soon as the competitor enters the competition area. A clear signal should then be given at the end of the run; this is usually an air horn or whistle. Organisers may vary the run timings but as long as they are consistent throughout the competition this will be fair.

Boundaries

Boundaries are very important to the competitors and the judges. The competitors need to know where the moves are to be performed and the judges need to know what exactly the competition area is. Most of the time, moves will only be scored when performed in the hole or on the wave. This is to discourage competitors endlessly cartwheeling down eddy lines and it also keeps the competition in good view of the judges. Some event organisers may change the boundaries to suit the water features; this is not a problem so long as everyone understands the area of competition.

It is advisable to keep areas such as eddies that are close to the competition site clear during the event, as competitors who get blown off the wave will need the space in which to travel back.

Water Conditions

Water conditions are very relevant to freestyle competition as different conditions can dictate different moves. It is important to find a site where the water conditions will remain constant throughout the event. This is not always possible as conditions can change easily, especially on tidal waters.

Who can Judge

There are no formal qualifications for judging freestyle but it won't be long before there are. At present people wishing to judge freestyle need to build up experience by attending events, and observing and working alongside established judges.

Most judges have a freestyle orientated background, however this is not essential. What is essential is an understanding and current knowledge of freestyle moves and developments. As a judge gains more 'eyes on' experience they will soon gain a good understanding of which moves link together and how to spot them coming; their scoring will also become more consistent and accurate.

River running is the future of freestyle...

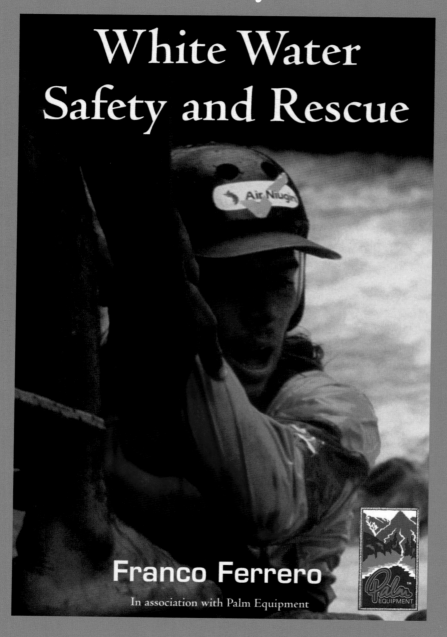

White Water Safety and Rescue

Franco Ferrero

In association with Palm Equipment

Reading this book may increase you life expectancy... considerably!

ISBN   0 - 9531956 - 0 - 0

Illustrations and Photos

Illustrations on pages 32 and 33 by Barney Caulfield of Palm International. Illustrations in chapters 9.1 and 9.3 by Lisa Ferrero.

All photographs that are not specifically acknowledged in the captions or in this appendix were taken by Tom Hughes.

Page	Paddler, Location	Photographer / Source
Front	Richard Chrimes, 99 Worlds, Full James NZ	Jason Smith / Pyranha
Back	Bill Mattos	Helen Metcalfe / Nookie
2	Greer Mackenzie, Colca Canyon, Peru	Tom Hughes
3	Shaun Baker, Colorado, USA	Darren Baker
4	(Top) Eric Brymer, India	Mitesh Makanjee
4	(Middle) Loel Collins	Tom Hughes
4	(Bottom) Tom Hughes	Small Nepali Child
5	Paul 'Cheesy' Robertson, California	Linda Gale / Pyranha
6	Thomas Rogenhoser, River Rhine	Horst Fürsattel / Pyranha
7	Tracey Clapp, Rock Island, Tennessee, USA	Pyranha archives
8	Simon Westgarth, Holme Pierpont, England	Jason Smith / Pyranha
9	Vicky Young, Augsburg	Pyranha archives
12	Deb Pinniger	Heather Gunn / Playboating Magazine
17	Paul 'Cheesy' Robertson, California	Linda Gale / Pyranha
22	'Fast' Eddy Cleaton, River Lothar, Austria	Paul 'Cheesy' Robertson
25	Pete Astles, River Inn, Austria	Pete Astles / Peak UK
31	Paul Cripps	Amazonas Explorer Rafting
34	Pete Astles, Skookumchuk, Canada	Matt Stepens / Peak UK
35	Matt Stephens, Skookumchuk, Canada	Pete Astles / Peak UK
41	Paddler Unknown, Full James, NZ	Jason Smith / Pyranha
42	Simon Westgarth, Holme Pierpont, England	Jason Smith / Palm
45	Franco Ferrero, Canolfan Tryweryn, Wales	Plas y Brenin
47	'Fast' Eddy Cleaton, River Lothar, Austria	Paul 'Cheesy' Robertson / Pyranha
51	Steve Whetman, Nookie's top secret test site	Helen Metcalfe / Nookie
56	Vicky Young, Augsburg, Germany	Pyranha archives
60	Tim Thomas, Cork, Ireland	Helen Metcalfe / Nookie
62	Bill Mattos / Nookie's top secret test site	Helen Metcalfe / Nookie
64	Bill Mattos	Helen Metcalfe / Nookie
68	Bill Mattos / Nookie's top secret test site	Helen Metcalfe / Nookie
71	Craig Dearing, River Etive, Scotland	Tom Hughes
75	Bleddyn Hughes, Canolfan Tryweryn, Wales	Bob Timms
79	Bill Mattos / Nookie's top secret test site	Helen Metcalfe / Nookie
83	Shaun Baker / Hurley Weir, UK	Darren Baker / Shaun Baker
84	Colin Hill, Minj, Papua New Guinea	Paul O'Sullivan
85	John 'Pies' Smith, Hurley Weir, England	Tom Hughes
89	Steve Whetman, Nookie's top secret test site	Helen Metcalfe / Nookie
92	Helen 'HT' Gould, 99 Worlds, NZ	Chris 'Jesus' Gould
93	Steve Whetman, Canolfan Tryweryn	Tom Hughes

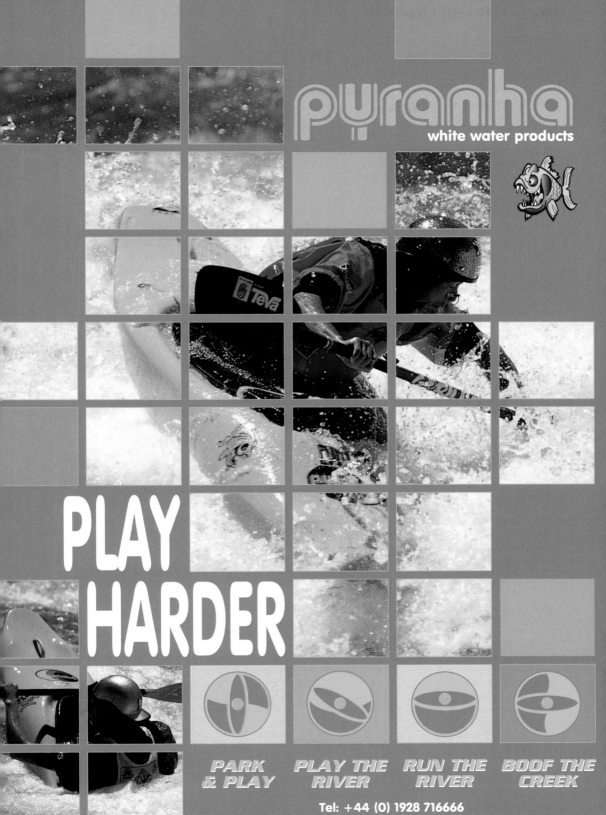

Index